THE 7 LAWS OF THE GOLF SWING

VISUALIZING THE PERFECT SWING TO MAXIMIZE YOUR GAME

NICK BRADLEY

Foreword by Justin Rose

Abrams, New York

Editor: Margaret L. Kaplan
Designer: Danielle Young
Production Manager: True Sims

Cataloging-in-Publication Data has been applied for and
may be obtained from the Library of Congress.

ISBN: 978-1-4197-0944-9

Printed and bound in China
10 9 8 7 6 5 4 3 2

Abrams books are available at special discounts when
purchased in quantity for premiums and promotions
as well as fundraising or educational use. Special editions
can also be created to specification. For details, contact
specialsales@abramsbooks.com or the address below.

THE ART OF BOOKS SINCE 1949

115 West 18th Street
New York, NY 10011
www.abramsbooks.com

CONTENTS

FOREWORD

JUSTIN ROSE, HAMPSHIRE, ENGLAND

I somehow cannot believe that it was over five years ago that Nick asked me to write the Foreword for *The 7 Laws of the Golf Swing*. I am glad to report that it has been massively popular, won awards and become one of the bestselling golf books this century! At the PGA and European Tour events Nick attended with me, there was rarely a time when I didn't see a golf fan shaking his hand to thank him for the birth of the 7 laws and tell him how it has benefited or saved their game.

I believe Nick managed to achieve that sometimes unobtainable combination in a book whereby you deliver a feeling and a strong image or concept in one hit. I know, having worked with Nick for three years, how valuable these images and concepts are for creating a framework that you can always revisit. Nick's concepts and images are based around common sense; they are formulated from the sound techniques of past champions that have worked so well in the past.

In any golf book there must be some text, but I have always felt that any wording should not distract from a strong image or feeling. (Now watch Nick bring out a book with just text!). Nick reduces the amount of description by bullet-pointing his way around the book and not delivering any more description or understanding than is genuinely needed. When you have a lesson with Nick, you experience less talk and more doing and thus more understanding through your body.

In November 2007, I had the chance to capture the European Tour Order of Merit title; to do this, I essentially had to win the Volvo Masters, the final and closing event on the tour. That week, Nick and I worked through some of the images and concepts from *The 7 Laws* that have served me well in the past. I particularly remember the 7-iron I hit into the 17th hole (one of the most treacherous green complexes in golf) to set up an essential birdie. Armed with some very simplistic feels, I went on to win the tournament and secure the order of merit. Sentences and reams of information are simply not what's needed in those pressured circumstances.

I know this new-look *7 Laws* will find its way into the hands of many golfers, beginners and pros alike. View it as your true north, a book to develop your swing from and to reference for when things are inconsistent. With Nick's concepts, I achieved one of my golfing dreams, and I have no doubt that *The 7 Laws* will improve your game too.

INTRODUCTION

Since its launch in 2003, I have been extremely proud and happy of the performance, comments and awards that *The 7 Laws of the Golf Swing* has gained. I have received and continue to receive emails from all corners of the golfing world. Golfers ranging from PGA Tour players to doctors have told me of the turnaround in their golf swings that's come from the structure that the book gave them. This book is primarily based around fundamentals that will always be present and remain as the "ground level" from which everything is built—at least until the physiology of the human body changes from its present biomechanical state. You may also find that *The 7 Laws* contains many "Eureka!" moments for you, since the rule of common sense runs strong through the text and the images. But as my mentor Colin Turner always says to me, "What is common sense is rarely common practice!"

I have discovered that people use books in different ways. Some will take snippets of information and "grow" themselves and their golf swings from sentences of insight. Others want the whole book thrown at them, and will study, dissect and install aspects of technique at their own learning speed. Many have commented on the imagery, relaying how they really have taken the killer "verbal" instruction away from their golfing experience. This is key. Let me tell you why.

Our imagination and visual representation of the golf swing is our biggest asset to improvement. I believe that the first step to creating massive change in a golfer's technique is to give the concept of change in a clear visual way; with a clear concept the brain can slowly move towards its goal. Unfortunately, we have seen several golfers through the years lose their pictures. The most graphic example is that of the Spanish genius Seve Ballesteros. No golfer could have been more visual and sensory than Seve, but the spoken English "verbal" instruction he became exposed to slowly and surely erased his pictures to a blank page. Seve only came "alive" again when he hit the ball amongst the trees, forcing him to conjure up a visual get-out-of-jail shot! So I urge you to gain your concepts through my pictures and develop your understanding through my text.

I was thrilled when Justin Rose wrote the foreword to the first edition of *The 7 Laws*, and this edition contains a new foreword by Justin, written from the perspective of a pupil of mine. I started coaching Justin during May 2006 soon after I moved to the USA, when he was 116th in the world rankings. What I saw at that time was a world-class golfer moving further away from the "truths" of the golf swing. In 2009 he was ranked as the sixth-best player in the world and was the European Tour Order of Merit Champion. It was a big turnaround to take in . . . even for my imagination.

Many of the philosophies that enabled Justin's transformation are contained within this book; we referred to them recently as reminders of fundamental motion. Like any individual wanting to make genuine improvement, the ability to be a great pupil is a key component, and this is certainly true of Justin Rose. I thoroughly enjoyed working with this consummate professional and I thank him for his commitment. Cheers, JR!

Whether you are a touring professional, a top amateur, a club golfer or a beginner, I know that *The 7 Laws* can give you the vision and concept of a great golf swing.

All the best,

LAW 1

THE GRIP
Naturally formed is neutrally performed

INTRODUCTION

Your level of success as a golfer is determined solely by the degree of control that you possess over the trajectory, direction and speed of the golf ball. In turn, the quality and efficiency of every physical action that you perform during your swing is largely determined by the quality of your grip formation in relation to the golf club.

There is no compromise when forming your grip; it either works in harmony with the club or it does not. In the same way that an artist will start with a rough, disorganized sketch and, in time, build on that initial outline to create a masterpiece, you must constantly refine your grip until it is at one with the club, body and mind. In short, exquisitely placed hands onto the golf club should be viewed as nothing less than a living work of art.

The hands are incredibly versatile instruments. They are sensitive to temperature, they assist you with your balance and they relay feelings of weight and texture. When playing golf, your grip carries this vital information to the brain and it is essential that

In more than 90 percent of instances, a faulty grip will create a damaging swing flaw.

the correct messages are able to filter through. A neutral grip is one that establishes total harmony between the clubface and the hands. When these two factors work in unison the potential of the golf swing can be realized. If your hands are poorly positioned in relation to your body and the club, the golf swing becomes suppressed, and is reduced to nothing more than a muddle of compensatory actions.

Unfortunately, the grip is a feature of the golf swing that can deteriorate over a period of time without offering any visible, telltale signs of doing so. The grip is usually one of the last things that a golfer considers when things start to go awry on the course, yet almost every move performed during the swing is affected by it in some way or other.

Although the importance of the mental aspect of the game cannot be overstated, as it is a vital component of playing great golf, physical errors can cripple even the most intelligent and mentally resilient athlete or sportsman. In my experience a faulty grip will create a damaging swing flaw in more than 90 percent of instances, and creating the correct grip-formation habits early on will save you plenty of time, work and frustration at a later stage in your golfing life.

An analogy may best explain why the grip is so crucial: imagine a race between a professional Formula One racing driver and your average road user. The Formula One driver draws the short straw and has to drive a conservative family sedan while the other driver is given a Ferrari.

Although the average driver would initially struggle to gain full control over the power of the Ferrari, they would still be able to achieve a decent level of competency relatively quickly. The Formula One driver, even with the added advantages of experience, knowledge and tactical skill, would inevitably find his performance restricted by the physical limitations of his car.

This chapter will show you how to take the first steps to creating a sound and consistent swing by building a solid grip that unifies the relationship between the handle of the club and the hands. Remember, a great golf swing shows expression, not suppression.

THE GRIP—SETTING THE COMPASS OF THE SWING

A key point that applies to all aspects of learning golf is that you should always focus on what you want to achieve rather than what you want to avoid. A neutral grip founded upon the body's natural biomechanical laws will enable you to achieve this, as it will provide you with a level of confidence and belief that will help stop the combination of negative self-talk, anxieties and doubts that can ruin your chances of playing well.

A NEUTRAL GRIP—A NATURAL TARGET.

A GRIP IN WHICH THE HANDS AND CLUB
ARE ONE IS THE PERFECT GRIP.

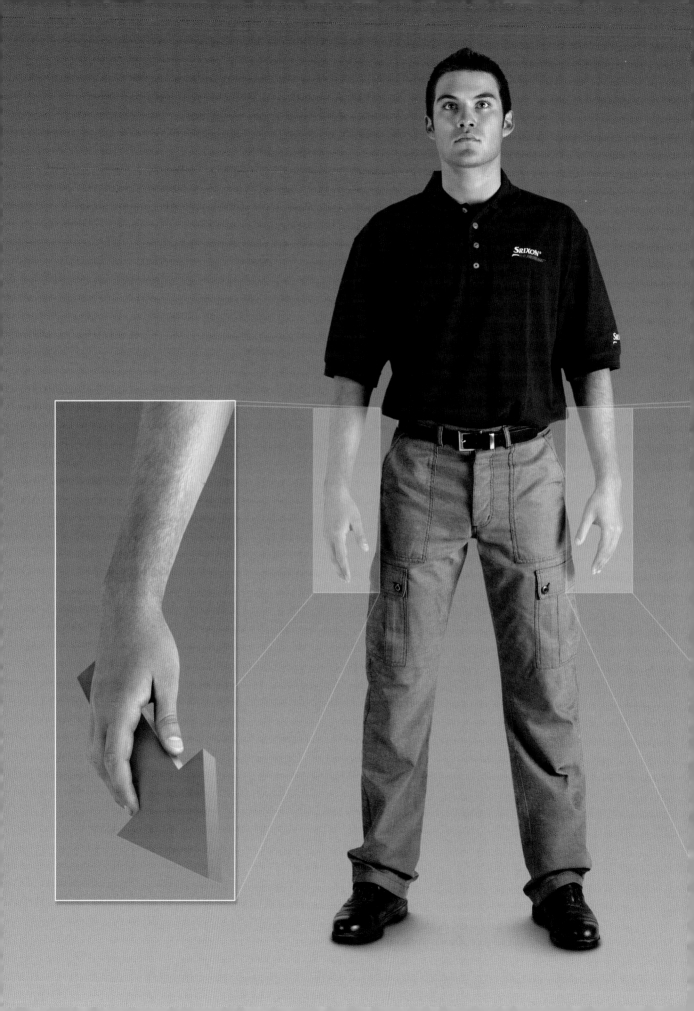

A neutral grip also has the benefit of instructing your eyes to automatically focus on what is a realistically achievable target instead of scanning and searching for a safe place to "miss" the shot. Everything that you read on the grip throughout the whole of this chapter is based upon two indisputable laws—the law of natural hand alignment and the law of mobility.

SUB-LAW 1: THE LAW OF NATURAL HAND ALIGNMENT

This law is based upon the fact that the human body is symmetrical in its structure. Both sub-laws pay particular attention to this fact, since the way in which you position your body when addressing the ball will either trigger a chain reaction of solid, orthodox and powerful moves or a series of power-sapping and inconsistent compensations.

Your grip is the starting point in the process of creating balance within the swing.

The further your swing moves away from the basics of symmetry and equality, the more it has to fight for consistency and simplicity. Your grip is the starting point in the process of creating balance within the swing.

The cornerstone of your whole grip is the theory that your hands should retain their natural positioning and alignment in relation to the body. As you see here, when the arms hang naturally from the shoulders, both palms turn inwards slightly towards the thighs.

It is essential that you maintain this natural positioning when placing your hands on the club in order to ensure total neutrality, with neither side of the body fighting for dominance. Adhering to the body's natural laws will give you the best possible chance of creating a grip routine that is both consistent and technically correct.

 AN ILLUSTRATION OF NATURAL HAND ALIGNMENT.

In order to hit the ball powerfully and accurately, your hands must be allowed to behave with total freedom of movement. One of the most destructive swing flaws is simply gripping the club too tightly—very often as an instinctive reaction to nerves or in response to a succession of poorly hit shots. When this occurs, the handle of the club often moves away from the base of the fingers and up into the palm of the hands. As you will discover, apart from robbing the wrists' freedom of motion, the golfer unwittingly creates a framework that has no potential or scope for significant improvement in the swing.

UNDERSTANDING THE CAPITATE JOINT AND WHY IT IS SO IMPORTANT TO YOUR GAME

The capitate joint is rarely mentioned in books outside of the medical profession, yet it is one of the key parts of the body for playing golf since it determines the degree of mobility and flexibility

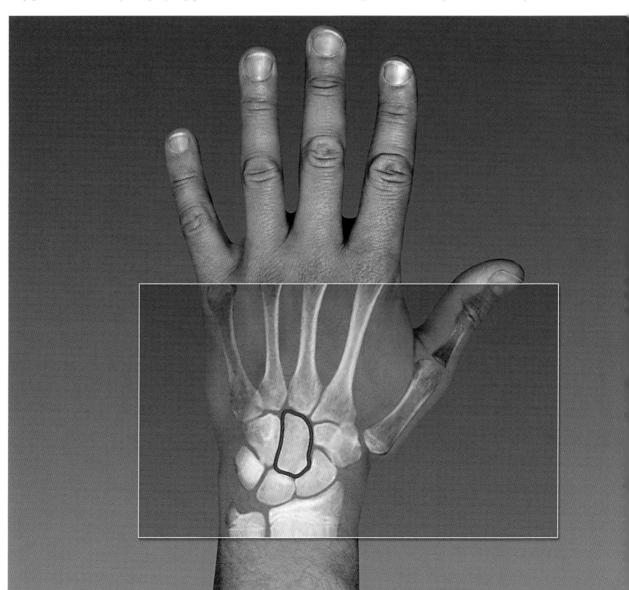

enjoyed by your hands and wrists. The relationship between the position of this joint and the handle of the club will determine the quality of your grip and with it your ability to generate power during the swing. As a general rule, the closer the handle of the club moves away from the base of the fingers and into the palm of the hand towards the capitate joint, the more restricted your wrist action will become. And, as you will probably have gathered by now, lack of freedom and mobility in the golf swing is almost always destructive.

The only time it is desirable to place the grip of the club high in the palm near the capitate joint is when you are looking to restrict your hand and wrist action, as you might on or around the putting green. Many Tour pros will position the putter grip right underneath the thumb pad in order to ensure that their wrists do not break during the stroke.

THE CAPITATE JOINT (HIGHLIGHTED IN RED) PLAYS
A KEY ROLE IN THE FORMATION OF GOOD GRIP.

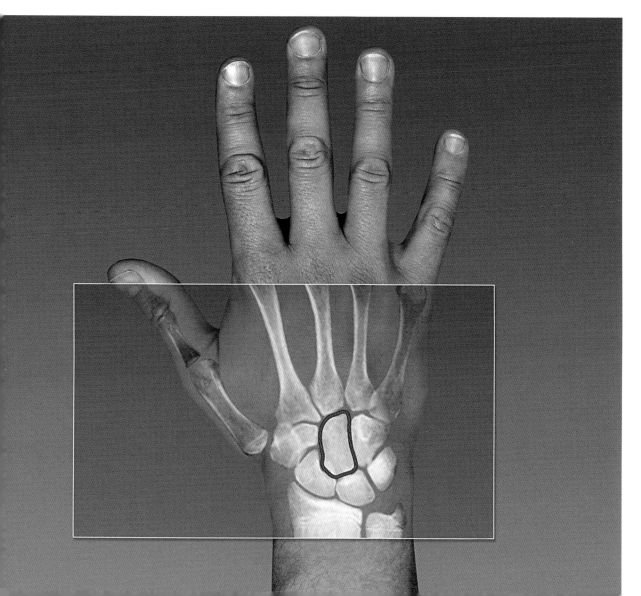

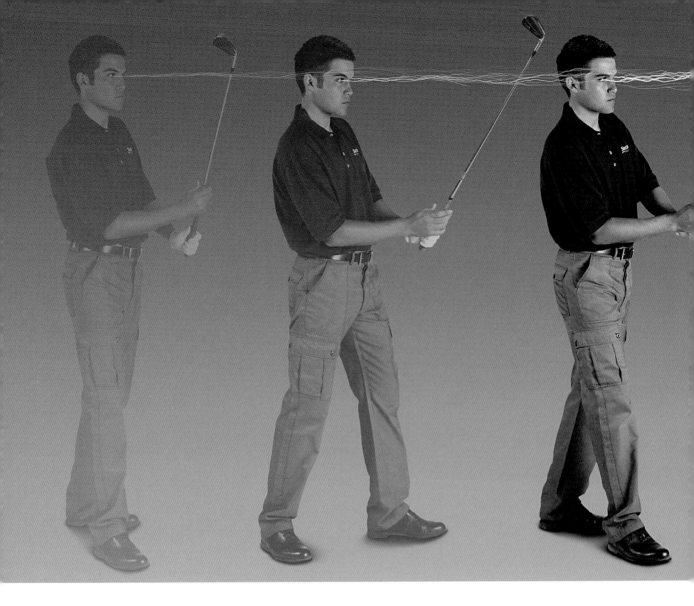

FORMING THE PERFECT GRIP—IT'S ALL DOWN TO THE ROUTINE

A precise and fundamentally correct grip is very difficult to achieve if your routine varies from shot to shot. Just as a lock on a door does not jump around to align itself to an incoming key, but is fixed, so the handle of the club should remain steady and still while the hands are carefully placed in position.

If you watch the world's top players, you will see that they are meticulous about the way in which they grip the club. Repeating the grip formation procedure in exactly the same way each time will maximize your chances of holding the club correctly and also guard against the bad habits and flaws that can creep into your game over a period of time.

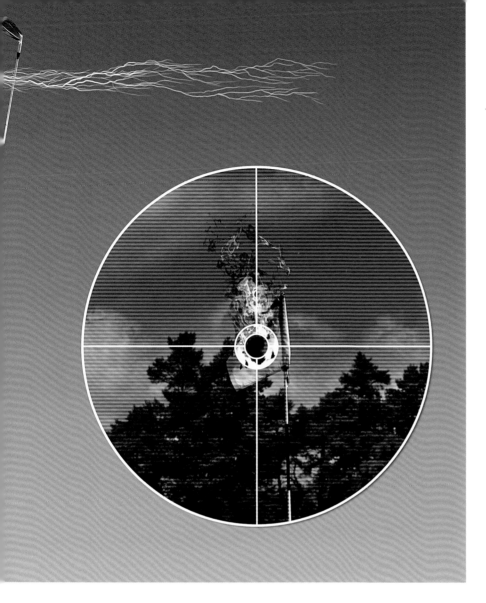

◀ FORMING YOUR
GRIP AWAY
FROM THE BALL
WILL HELP YOU
FOCUS ON YOUR
TECHNIQUE.

FORM YOUR GRIP AWAY FROM THE BALL AND IN FRONT OF YOUR BODY

Placing your hands on the golf club is the last action that requires conscious thought before you start your swing. The completion of your grip is the trigger that starts your pre-shot routine, which will be an instinctive and spontaneous series of movements that require you to think of nothing else other than the shot you want to hit.

For this reason, it is important that you form your grip away from the ball so that you can concentrate on getting your grip technique right before you allow yourself to slip into your subconscious mode of thought.

The completion of your grip is the trigger that starts your pre-shot routine.

THE PERFECT LEFT HAND DELIVERY

Because your palms naturally turn inwards slightly, delivering the club into the left hand at a 45-degree north-easterly angle allows the shaft to align itself perfectly to the angle of the left hand. I recommend that you perform this part of the routine while directly facing your target, as this will provide the best perspective of the shot and also give the whole routine a foundation or point of reference.

There are many instances in every-day life that mirror the way that the handle of the club is delivered into the left hand. The most accurate of these is the way that the handlebars on a motor bike are positioned. Each handle is positioned at a 45-degree angle to complement the natural physiology of the forearms and this, in turn, provides the rider with the most comfortable, natural and effective way of controlling the bike.

YOU SHOULD INTRODUCE THE ▶
CLUB FROM A 45-DEGREE
NORTH-EASTERLY ANGLE.

KEY GRIP FLAW—THE LONG LEFT THUMB

This is one of the most common and most destructive grip flaws. Extending the left thumb down the handle of the grip causes several problems and has many damaging effects in the swing. The left hand, wrist and forearm act as shock absorbers through impact as the club-head strikes the turf. When the left thumb is placed in the correct position, the tendons in your hands have the ability to flex, bounce and withstand this force. However, when the left thumb is in an elongated position, the tendons in the left hand become stretched, taut and susceptible to injury, especially if the golfer is holding the club too tightly—an automatic knock-on effect of the long left thumb.

The long left thumb also damages the pincer or trigger formation that should be created with your left index finger and thumb, thereby forfeiting control and power during the swing. Thirdly, it forces the grip away from the fingers and into the palm of the left hand.

THE DELIVERY OF THE RIGHT HAND

Apart from introducing the handle of the club into the left hand, the right hand can still perform three vital functions for grip perfection:

FUNCTION 1: PREVENT THE LONG LEFT THUMB

As soon as the right hand has presented the club to the left, you can guard against the long left thumb fault by pushing the shaft away from the body with the right hand while at the same time drawing the thumb up the shaft. In doing so, the left index finger also assumes a different position. It moves from under the shaft to the side. The thumb and the index finger now virtually oppose each other to create the pincer or trigger formation that is fundamental to gripping the club correctly.

FUNCTION 2: NESTLE THE CLUB AWAY FROM THE PALM INTO THE FINGERS

The right hand also has a role to play in preventing the handle of the club from resting too high in the palm of the left hand. As I mentioned earlier, gripping the club too much in the palm will restrict the mobility in your hands, wrists and forearms and prevent you from creating full power, leverage and accuracy.

PUSH THE SHAFT AWAY, AND DRAW THE THUMB UP.

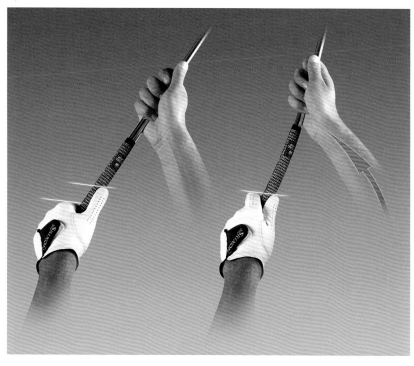

With your right hand still at the base of the handle, you can subtly draw the clubhead up towards the body. As you do this, feel that the handle works its way down into the fingers. Once you have practiced this a few times, you will soon be able to draw the left thumb up and push the handle of the grip down as you are focusing on your target. I promise you that it won't be too long before it feels perfectly natural to stand behind the ball and "size up" your target as you do this. The whole process can be distilled down to just a couple of very valuable seconds.

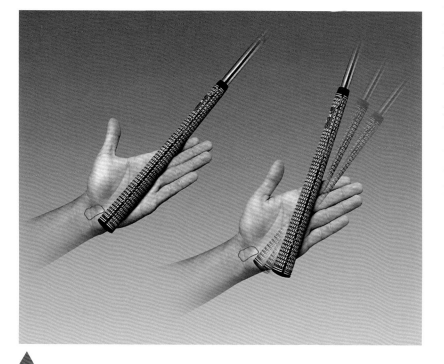

AVOID THE PALM AND FAVOR THE FINGERS.

FUNCTION 3: CREATE POSITIONAL EQUALITY

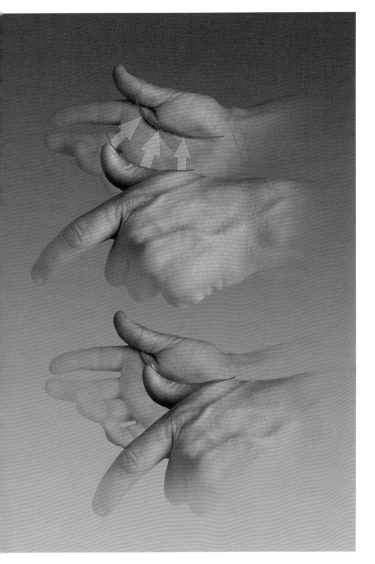

The right hand approaches the left from above in order to provide a visual point of reference for creating a mirror image of the left hand. To unite the hands on the grip, dock the left thumb into the crevice formed between the lifeline and thumb pad of your right hand and apply an authoritative downward pressure with the right hand. **This is the most important link of the hands**. If positioned correctly, the right hand will touch more of the left hand than the club itself. In fact, the only parts of the right hand that should touch the golf club are the fingers. Holding the grip in the base of the fingers like this enables you to avoid the disastrous act of interfering with the capitate joint and instead gives the hands a full range of movement.

▲

DOCK THE LEFT THUMB INTO THE RIGHT HAND.

USE THIS IMAGE TO GET A FEELING
OF TRULY UNITING THE HANDS.

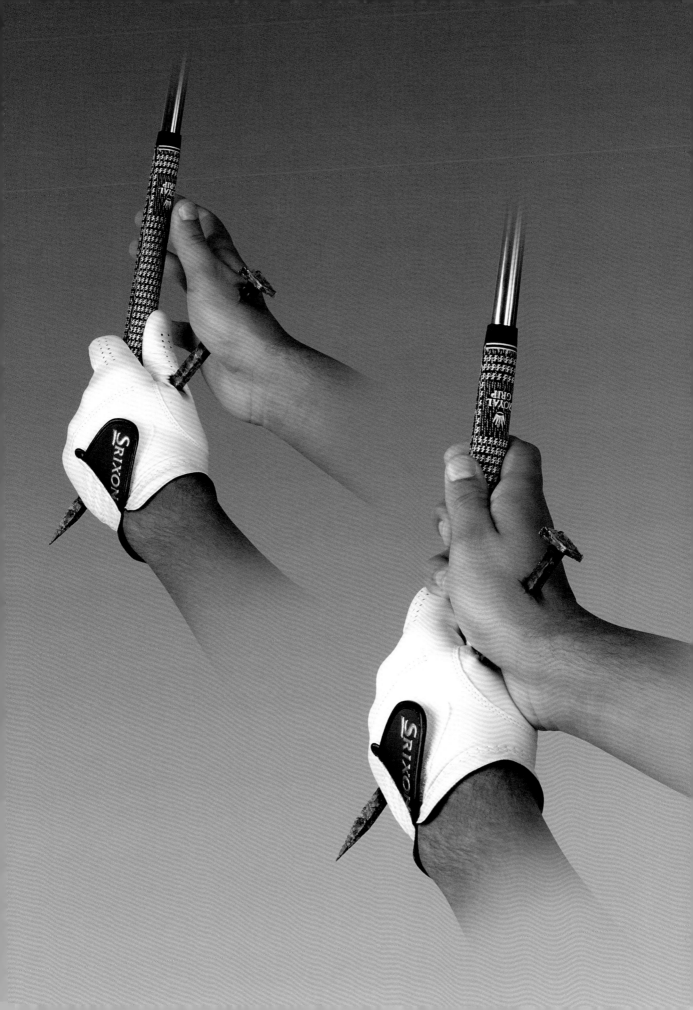

CREATING PINCER FORMATIONS

Every single day we unconsciously use our hands and fingers in a multitude of different ways. The pincer position, formed when the index finger and thumb are pressed together in a pinching fashion, would undoubtedly win the "most-used" category.

This action enables your hands to assert authority over anything they hold, lift, place or, indeed, pinch. Without the ability to form this position, our hands would be rendered virtually useless.

To achieve this vital pincer formation, it is imperative that both hands are positioned correctly on the club. It is, for example, physically impossible to create a pincer between the index finger and thumb of the left hand if the left thumb is positioned too far down the club. When the left thumb assumes this long and lazy position, the index finger retracts under the shaft to form a fist rendering it totally useless. As a result, none of the fingers on the left hand can apply any pressure to the grip.

Poor positioning of the right hand can also lead to the pincer position being forsaken. If the right hand approaches the grip from the side, instead of from above, it is highly likely that the club will be held in a "claw" fashion commonly associated with hooking the ball.

This image highlights the feeling that you should be looking to achieve at the completion of the grip. Take a club in your hand and pinch it, just as you would if you wanted to squirt the paint out of these tubes. It is this pressure and positioning that you want to recreate when gripping the club.

◀ A DEPICTION OF THE IDEAL PINCER PRESSURE.

JOINING HANDS IN HARMONY

There are several different options available to you when deciding on how to link your hands together on the grip. Each has its own advantages and disadvantages and the most suitable method for you is determined largely by the degree of strength and flexibility in your hands as well as their size. Let's have a look at each grip in a little more detail:

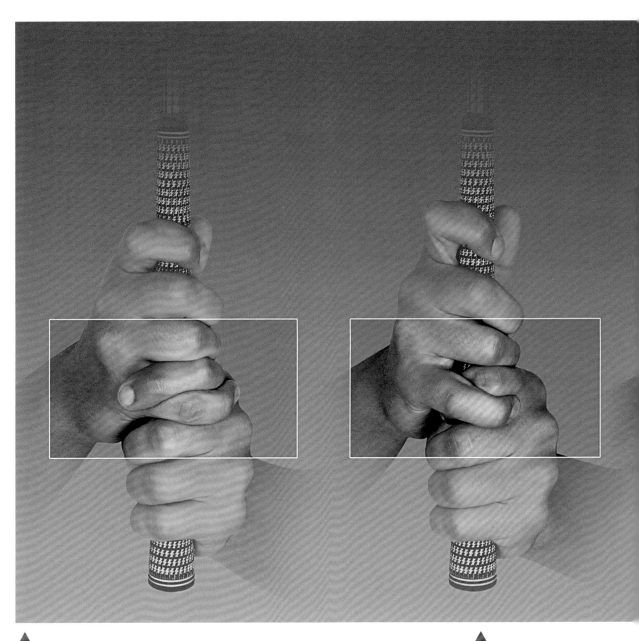

▲ INTERLOCK—INDUCED STRENGTH.

▲ OVERLAPPING—MOBILE AND VERSATILE.

INTERLOCKING

The Interlocking grip is a strength-inducing grip. If a golfer has neither the strength nor the suppleness to form the overlap or the intermesh, the Interlock can provide the answer. With this grip the player intertwines the little finger of the right hand and the index finger of the left to provide a formidable bond. While this version of the grip can limit the variety of shots the golfer has at his or her disposal, the benefits are found in the discipline it imposes. This grip suits medium to small hands.

OVERLAPPING

The Overlapping or "Vardon" grip provides the golfer with a linkage between the hands that is relatively easy to perform and use. As you will note, the little finger of the right hand sits diagonally on top of the left-hand index finger. I think of this as an artist's grip, since it lends itself to greater mobility, heightened feel, superb clubhead control, creativity and flair. This grip is suitable for players with medium to strong hands of an average size.

INTERMESH

The Intermesh grip is a compromise between the overlap and the interlock. It is formed by slotting the little finger of the right hand between the index and middle finger of the left hand. The key benefit of this particular grip is that all of the digits on each hand are in contact with the golf club, but it also allows the golfer to spread the hands further down the grip, gaining greater control. This grip suits the golfer who is caught between the interlock and the overlap.

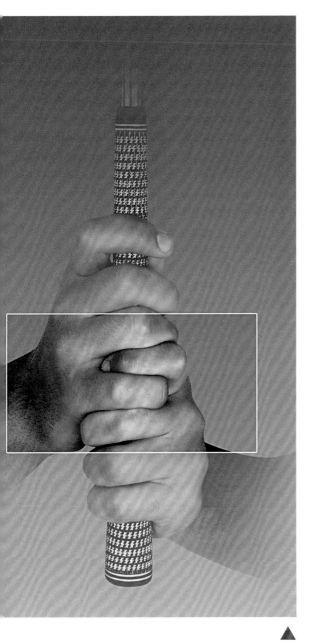

INTERMESH—ALL TEN FINGERS AND A LINK.

GRIP PRESSURE—LET THE GAS ESCAPE

The pressure applied by the hands to the handle of the golf club is an almost invisible aspect of swing technique. Not only is grip pressure a variable that is difficult to detect by an observer, it can very often avoid detection by the player in question as he or she becomes accustomed to holding the club either too tightly or too gently over a period of time.

Later in the book, in Law 4, I will highlight the problems that overly tight or loose grip pressure can create during the swing, but for the time being it is important to look at the optimum grip pressure.

This image of gas being allowed to seep liberally through the hands and escape from the inside of the grip highlights the perfect balance between tightness and slackness. The players with the best grips have always nurtured the handle of the club as a method of gaining the utmost sensation and feedback between the body and the mind. If you keep this image in mind, it will prove very useful when judging the pressure of your grip. Think of it this way—gripping the club with no authority whatsoever will allow a deluge of gas to escape from within. At the other end of the scale, if you strangle the club, no gas at all will be able to escape.

Both of the above faults are equally damaging in their own right. A good grip can crumble when authoritative pressure is absent. In most instances, the right hand usually starts to drop underneath the shaft as the left hand disintegrates into a weak position, where the handle of the club sits too high in the palm of the hand.

The tight grip, on the other hand, is the most difficult to detect because it rarely shows any visible signs of falling apart. Squeezing the handle too tightly—a difficult flaw to identify because the grip very often will appear perfectly orthodox from the outside, causes you to lose your appreciation of the weight in the clubhead and, in turn, your feel for the shot. An excessively tight grip will also prevent your wrists from hinging correctly, thereby destroying your ability to create power and leverage during the swing.

THE GAS CAN ESCAPE EVENLY WITH OPTIMUM GRIP PRESSURE.

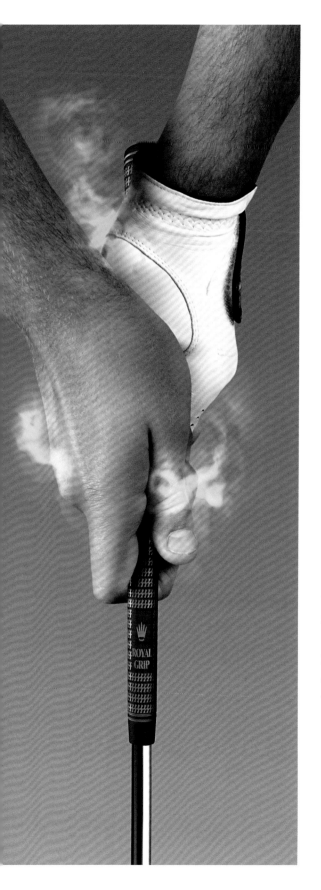

SUMMARY

If you take just one lesson away from the whole of this book, it should be that your golf swing is a reflection of your grip. The solution should always be to fix the engine first and then the bodywork.

However, it would be remiss of me to lead you into believing that making a grip change is an easy process. In the early stages of a change, your grip may very well feel awkward and uncomfortable, the ball may fly off in a different direction than normal and your game may suffer and your confidence may dip for a period of time while your body adjusts to your new hold on the club and as it subconsciously begins to realize that it no longer has to compromise good movement. The fight is over.

The acid test for your grip can be found in the amount of sidespin imparted onto the ball. Although there will inevitably be occasions when it is pertinent to look at a golfer's body motion, shots that severely slice or hook are crying out for a grip review. But you should always remember that any attempt to make an improvement to your technique is futile unless your hands can repeat their natural hanging positions from the body as they are placed onto the club. The grip is your link between your mind and the club. The quality of this relationship is determined by how well you hold the club.

Now that the hands are uniformly positioned on the club, we can look at the larger structure that houses the grip in Law 2—The Geometry of the Set-up.

LAW 2

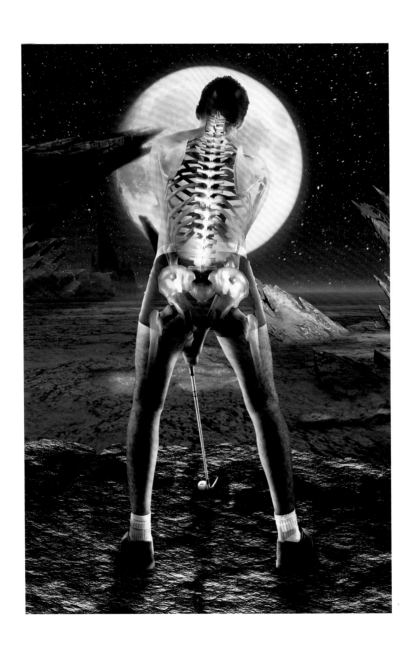

THE GEOMETRY OF THE SET-UP
Building stability from the ground upwards

INTRODUCTION

In the first chapter, I illustrated how the grip is the compass of the golf swing. However, since you do not strike the golf ball with your hands alone, your grip must be housed within a much larger structure in order to operate effectively and efficiently. This structure is your set-up position at address.

In forming your grip, you create a formula that offers a steadfast performance guarantee: if your hands mesh together on the club in a totally natural way, your grip will perform well. However, if your hand placement is haphazard, awkward or unorthodox, then your grip will perform poorly. It really is that simple.

Building your grip around the natural biomechanical alignment of your hands and forearms gives you a solid foundation and consistency in your swing that you can rely on from the outset. However, for your hands and arms to create a consistent motion, they must also have a platform or a base that can provide stability. The thin branches of a tree, for example, can only sway to and fro in the wind because they are linked to a solid trunk. Similarly the sails on a windmill can only rotate consistently because they are fixed and attached to the outside of the building.

A solid, powerful and consistent golf swing is only achievable if it, too, has a solid base able to control and harness the power.

A solid, powerful and consistent golf swing is only achievable if it, too, has a solid base able to control and harness the power. That base is the ground, and for that reason I will be explaining how and why, in conjunction with building the correct grip, the ground itself is of fundamental importance and is your starting point when developing your set-up and swing.

This chapter will examine in detail how you can build a solid address position, but before we start, one quick piece of advice: in order to become proficient at achieving the correct stance and posture at address, I highly recommend, if not insist, that you use a mirror to check your positioning. Throughout the entire golf learning process, you will find yourself continually misled and betrayed by your swing thoughts and feelings. A visual record is always the most accurate reference when learning all aspects of the swing and is particularly beneficial in forming the orthodox address position that will support a powerful and consistent swing motion.

UNDERSTANDING THE ROAD MAP OF YOUR SWING

Before you immerse yourself in the finer details of the set-up, take a moment to familiarize yourself with the chart below. This is your road map—or flow chart—for the golf swing and it shows you how, working back from the clubface, each key element of the swing is dependent on a larger, more powerful part of the body to provide support and stability. Therefore, in conjunction with building the correct grip, the ground is of fundamental importance when developing and maintaining your swing.

The Clubface is dependent on the Hands

The Hands are dependent on the Arms

The Arms are dependent on the Torso

The Torso is dependent on the Legs

The Legs are dependent on the Ground

The Ground is your Constant

GAIN STRENGTH FROM STABILITY BY ASSUMING A SET-UP THAT ▶
ADHERES TO THE BODY'S NATURAL STRUCTURAL COMPOSITION.

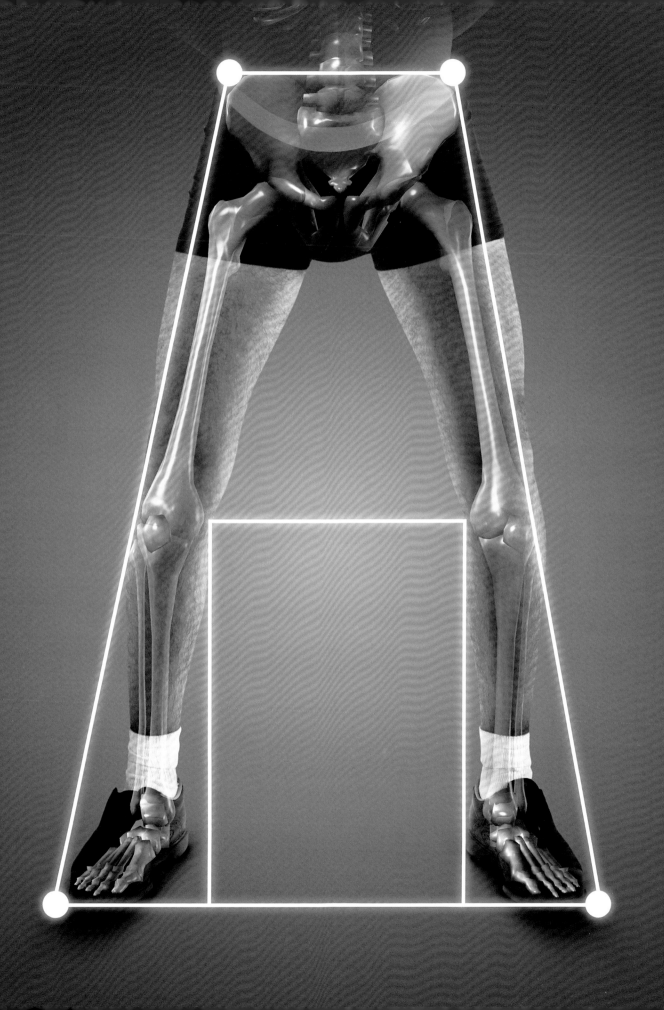

THE TRIANGULAR RELATIONSHIP OF THE SET-UP

A golf swing generates a tremendous amount of speed, torque and power. The role of the set-up is to provide a platform or base that is structurally sound enough to combine both discipline and efficiency with total freedom of movement. As with the formation of the grip that we looked at in the previous chapter, it is also very important to adhere to the body's basic structural composition when creating your set-up. When this is achieved, the feet, hips and legs, when placed into their most stable and balanced position, create a triangular shape, while the body itself appears virtually symmetrical in its composition.

SPLAYING THE FEET GIVES THE KNEES ROOM TO TURN

Study the image on page 33. The first detail to notice is how each foot is turned outwards at approximately 30 degrees from square. Splaying both feet a little enables the knees to move and rotate into a position where they are positioned directly above each foot. This is the strongest and most powerful leg structure possible.

When the mid-section in the body—located just above the hips—begins to rotate during the backswing, it creates a "ripple" effect that transfers throughout the lower body. The knees will instinctively follow suit and partially rotate, but if the feet remain square (pointing straight forward), there is nowhere for them to go. The end result can be disastrous because the knees are then forced to detour and bust out of the natural boundaries of the stance. As the support of the feet, knees and legs buckles, the torso will tilt or slide laterally instead of turning, altering many vital aspects of the swing dynamics.

As you position your knees at address, allow them to subtly follow the lead of the feet until you achieve a slight "squatting" appearance. Once this has been achieved, you should be aware of a slight resistance on the inside of each leg.

BALL POSITION—NOTHING MORE THAN A FLEETING MOMENT

Ball position may seem like an innocuous and relatively unimportant aspect of the set-up, but it influences many key elements of the golf swing, most notably the swing plane and path, the level of clubface activity at impact, not to mention the trajectory of the shot and the quality of the strike.

In the same way that the moon will only eclipse and hide the sun completely when alignment is perfect, so the clubface will only be able to squarely enter and exit the impact area and strike the ball powerfully when it is located in the correct position within the stance. Since every body is built differently, there is no one perfect ball position for every single golfer. Trial and error is part of the process of locating your ideal hitting area.

LEFT ARM DICTATES OPTIMUM BALL POSITION

Each golf club has a slightly different make-up in terms of the length of the shaft, the lie angle and the amount of loft on the clubface. It is only when the shaft of the club is vertical and the sole of the club is flush to the ground that these design features are accurately represented at address.

Your role during the golf swing is to create that perfect lie angle at the set-up stage and then later in the swing at impact when the left arm and the clubshaft reach their maximum length. When this happens the physical characteristics of the club—the shaft length, loft and lie angle—are restored to the form they took at the set-up. Keeping this simple fact in mind, the optimum ball position will be directly below your left armpit at address.

For most golfers, this will position the ball within a region of two to three inches to the right of the left heel. This relationship is a constant element of your set-up and the distance between the golf ball and the left heel must not vary to any great degree.

WHY A VARIABLE BALL POSITION WILL LEAD TO INCONSISTENCY

Shifting the ball position in your stance to accommodate clubs with different length and lofts will cause the natural design characteristics of that particular golf club to change. For example, it is often said that shorter irons require a more descending attack into the ball and, in view of this, many golfers will play the ball further back in their stance to achieve a steeper downswing. However, as the clubhead and the ball move to the right in the stance, the hands and arms remain in their natural free-hanging position, which is now well ahead of the ball. This removes loft from the clubface and causes it to assume a closed position, aiming left of the target.

The reverse is true when hitting a driver. Because golfers have been told so often that a shallow, sweeping blow is required to strike the ball slightly on the upswing, many golfers shift the ball too far forward in their stance. This time, when the hands and arms remain in their normal free-hanging position, they are too far behind the ball. The result is that the clubface is too open (aiming right) at address and too lofted, which is why so many amateur golfers consistently hit high slices off the tee.

LEARN FROM YOUR DIVOT PATTERNS

Good impact and ball position constitute nothing more than a brief moment in time when the clubhead is traveling along the ground for its longest and lowest period. Coupled with the correct body motion and swing plane, your divot pattern should be relatively long and shallow. If your divots are either too deep or too short, you may need to review your ball position.

WHERE THE RIGHT FOOT MOVES, THE STERNUM FOLLOWS

Although the relationship in terms of the distance between the ball and your left foot at address should remain consistent regardless of the club you are using, you can vary the position of the right foot to either increase the width of the stance to add stability to the set-up when using longer clubs or to narrow the stance when hitting shorter irons, such as wedges.

However, the key lesson to learn is that while your right foot is free to move, it is crucial that your sternum (chest bone) moves with it because it represents the body's center of gravity. When hitting a driver, for example, the clubface needs to strike the ball ever so slightly on the upswing, so the ball should be played slightly ahead of the sternum. However, if you then narrowed your stance to hit a pitching wedge simply by moving your right foot closer to the left, for example, your sternum would be way behind the ball, making it impossible to achieve the slight descending blow that is ideal for short irons. Therefore, in order to achieve the correct set-up position for your pitching wedge, you would need to move your right foot to the left and also move your upper body into a position where your sternum is marginally ahead of the ball.

The same principle applies when moving from the shorter irons to the longer clubs. Simply moving your right foot to increase the width of your stance to hit a driver, for example, will not produce the desired effect if your sternum remains in the same position as it was when hitting the pitching wedge, since it would create an excessively steep downswing.

To obtain a clear understanding of the relationship between the right foot and the sternum, take a close look at the following three diagrams:

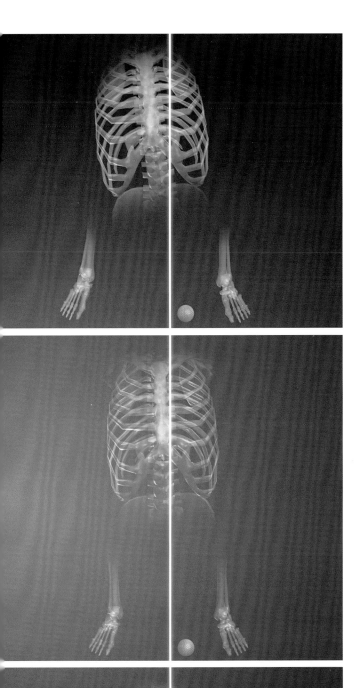

 MAXIMUM TILT—A SWEEPING
AND ASCENDING STRIKE.
(DRIVER AND LONG IRON)

◀ MARGINAL TILT—SHALLOW,
PIERCING AND SQUEEZED.
(MID-IRONS)

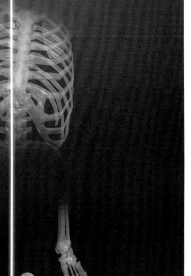 ◀ FRONTAL TILT—COMPRESSIVE
CONTACT. (SHORT IRONS
AND WEDGES)

Note: The only time that your right
foot should be positioned closer to the
ball than your right hip is when hitting
shots where there is a displacement
of weight forwards at address, such as
a chip shot or a low punch shot.

PERFECT POSTURE—STRONG AND GROUNDED, LIVELY AND ENERGIZED

Any object that moves at a very high speed, such as a Formula One car, can be controlled more easily when the center of gravity is low to the ground. Most golfers, and especially those over six feet tall, will need to lower their center of gravity to gain greater consistency and solidity at address and during the swing. A good posture allows you to achieve this and also to create a solid base to the swing and provide a foundation for the optimum swing plane.

I often refer to the spine as the coat hanger of the body because when it is straight and "angular," it creates a look and feeling of strength and athleticism in the upper body that is simply not achievable when in a curved and "soft" position.

Watch a weightlifter as he prepares to hoist a huge weight, a karate expert getting ready to punch, or a tennis player anticipating a serve and you will see how the body naturally prepares itself for action. The natural posture in this state of anticipation is strong and grounded, yet at the same time lively and energized. Golf is no exception.

TWO KEY CURVES TO PRESERVE

In all of the above sports, it is easy to incur an injury if the natural shape of the spine is replaced by a rounded, lazy posture. Having said that, there are two subtle key curves that you need to preserve when addressing the ball—one at the back of the neck and the other at the base of the spine. If either of these two curves is allowed to deteriorate, the spine will sag and slump under the weight of the torso.

Curve 1: The base of the spine

In order to create the angle in the spine that determines the body plane of your golf swing, the hips must contain a certain degree of pitch at address. This is achieved by slightly raising the coccyx at the very base of the spine.

Curve 2: Behind the neck

Lifting your chin away from your chest at address gives your shoulders the room and freedom to rotate through 90 degrees around your spine angle.

◀ MAINTAIN THE UPPER-NECK AND TAILBONE CURVES.

HOW POOR BODY POSITIONING CAN AFFECT YOUR BALANCE

The quality of your posture determines the quality of the body and club motion during the swing. The torso is the catalyst of this motion and since it is the "middle ground" of the body, it has a direct influence on how both the upper and lower body behave. Your torso is the key to your balance—good or bad—quite simply because it represents your whole body's center of gravity.

The cause of a loss of balance can more often than not be traced back to an anomaly at address and, in particular, to poor positioning of the mid-section of the body. Most of the damage created by this set-up flaw manifests itself in the downswing when the trunk is unwinding at speed and creating huge amounts of centrifugal force.

Make sure that your weight is positioned somewhere between your heels and the balls of your feet.

If your weight is placed too far towards your toes at address, your weight will inevitably be thrown forwards and outwards by the rotational force generated in the downswing. If, however, your weight is set back towards your heels, the momentum of the downswing movement will throw you backwards and laterally to the side during the downswing.

As you form your address, stance and posture, make sure that your weight is positioned somewhere between your heels and the balls of your feet. Use this image to reinforce what is one of the most important elements of the golf swing.

THE ALL-IMPORTANT MIDDLE GROUND OF THE GOLF SWING. ▶

THE DORSAL ASPECT OF THE SET-UP

In order to give your upper body the best possible chance to rotate around your spine instead of tilting, it is important that your right hip and shoulder are positioned slightly lower than the left at address. Although this shift from the perpendicular is only very subtle, you should feel a slight lifting of the left hip as your spine tilts away from the target. This small tilt will automatically allow your weight to transfer onto your right side as you coil your upper body around the axis of the spine.

The position is completed when the spine, sternum and nose complete a straight line. Structurally this image makes perfect biomechanical sense. The spine has assumed a linear look from top to bottom with no unwanted curves or tilts. Remember, to wind it, you must be behind it.

THE DISASTROUS SCOLIOSIS EFFECT

Scoliosis is a condition of the spine that even those with an untrained medical eye will be able to see from the image overleaf. The unwanted spinal curvature could prevent your upper body from turning fully and seriously reduce your ability to pivot correctly in the backswing. In fact, the condition is a common cause of one of the most destructive backswing faults—the reverse pivot, where the weight remains fixed on the front foot during the backswing.

The first key difference between this and the correct dorsal aspect of the set-up can be found in the right hip, which is set considerably higher than the left. You can also see that the spine snakes in the middle section of the back, pushing the whole body mass onto the left foot. The crucial effect of this poor spinal alignment is that the high right hip creates a "blocking" effect, where it simply refuses to allow anything to pass. Since it cannot turn, the right hip tilts even higher during the backswing, which makes a level and powerful upper body coil all but impossible to achieve.

It is worth remembering that most of us will suffer from a bad back at some point during our lives. Prevention is always better than cure and so it is advisable to visit a reputable osteopath once every three to six months to prevent back problems occurring and to alleviate scoliosis if you do have it.

◀ A SAFE AND STRUCTURALLY SOUND SET-UP POSITION.

A QUICK SCOLIOSIS CHECK
FOR THE RIGHT-HANDED GOLFER

For a quick check to see if scoliosis is present, look down towards your navel. If it is positioned significantly to the right of your sternum it is worth paying a visit to a reputable osteopath. Similarly, if you stand with your left foot naturally turned outwards, it is likely that you may be suffering from the effects of scoliosis without even realizing it.

THIS IMAGE OF A GOLFER AND THE BARREL REPRESENTATION OF THE UPPER, MID- AND LOWER SECTIONS OF THE BODY SHOW THE DISASTROUS EFFECTS OF SCOLIOSIS.

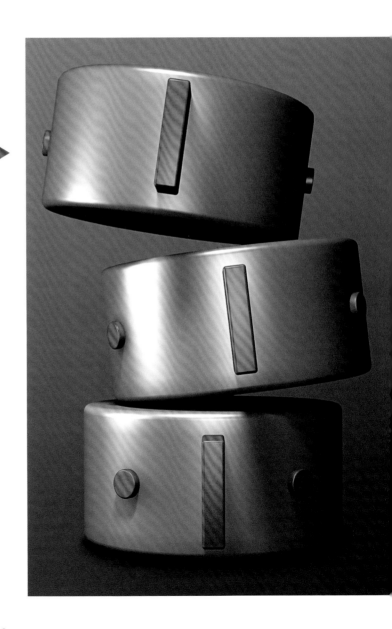

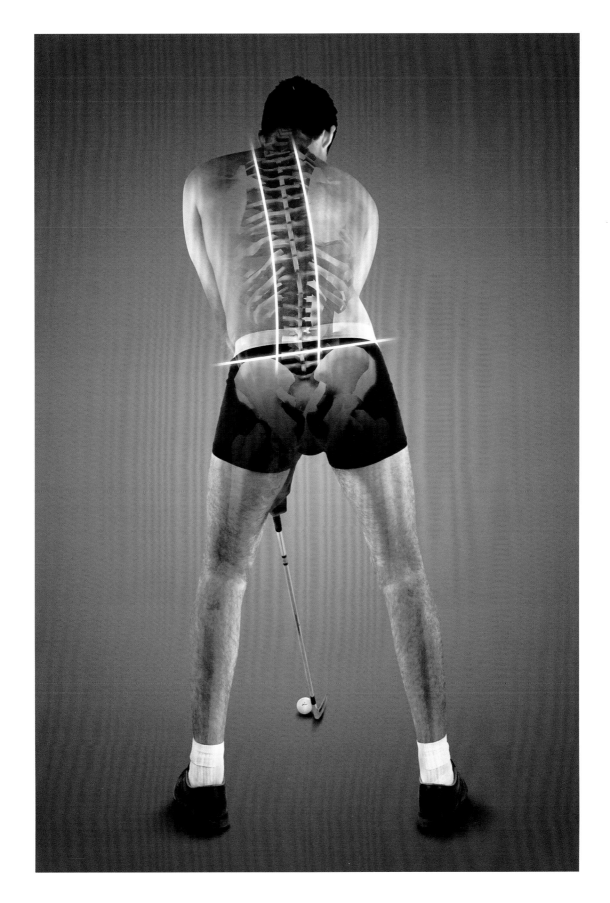

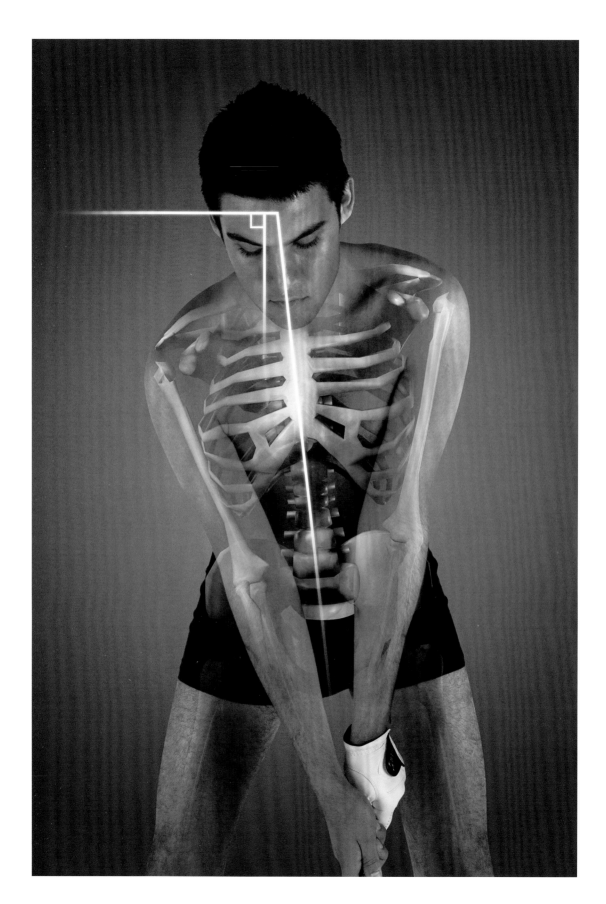

TORQUE 1—CREATING BIOMECHANICAL EFFICIENCY AT ADDRESS

In the ideal set-up position, your nose, sternum and spine should be aligned perfectly with each other. The relationship between the position of your head and your sternum at address serves three very important functions before and during the golf swing:

FUNCTION 1: TO COMPLETE THE ALIGNMENT OF THE SPINE

Keeping your nose and sternum in a straight line completes the alignment of the spine from the base of the lower back to the top of your head, thereby creating a safe and structurally sound position. Ensuring that the spine is straight reduces the risk of injury and removes unwanted strain on the spine, neck and shoulder joints.

FUNCTION 2: TILTED SPINE ANGLE PRESETS WEIGHT TRANSFERENCE

As your nose, sternum and spine complete their linear structure, your upper body will naturally tilt away from the target thus creating biomechanical efficiency. Your upper body will now be able to pivot around this pole, while the slightly angled position automatically facilitates the correct weight transference in the backswing by creating a slightly tilted axis around which the torso can rotate.

FUNCTION 3: PREVENTION OF AN EARLY TURN

One of the most common and destructive swing faults is allowing your body to turn too early. During the golf swing, the clubhead has a greater distance to travel than any other moving part of the body. In order for the hands, arms, shoulders, hips and knees to rendezvous at the top of the backswing and then again at impact at the same time, the clubhead must move faster than the rest of the body.

The correct alignment of the nose, sternum and spine governs the motion of the golf swing by preventing the upper body from turning too quickly during the takeaway and, in doing so, assists greatly in the general timing of the swing by ensuring that the clubhead has a chance to make an early start.

◀ TORQUE 1—NOTICE THE ALIGNMENT OF NOSE, STERNUM AND SPINE.

LINKING YOUR ARMS TO YOUR BODY

The importance of linking the smaller, more variable parts to a larger whole has been a continual theme throughout this chapter and nowhere is this philosophy more relevant than when high-lighting the relationship between your arms and your body at address.

Just as the planet Earth provides the Moon with a stable fixture around which it can consistently orbit, the sheer mass and size of your torso provides your arms with a great source of perma-nence, consistency, reliability and control.

THINK ELBOWS TO HIPS AT ADDRESS

A link—or fusion—between the body and arms is an essential aspect of the golf swing. You create this linkage by turning your arms outwards slightly so that your elbow joints point at their corresponding hip joints. If you do this correctly, your arms will literally hang off from the upper part of your chest and gently sandwich your golf shirt between your upper arms and your body. This serves two functions:

FUNCTION 1: ALLOWS RIGHT ARM TO FOLD CORRECTLY

Positioning your right elbow joint so that it points toward the right hip at address will allow your right arm to fold at the elbow during your backswing like a hinge on a door, while the upper part of the arm remains fairly close to your chest and torso. At the start of the downswing, your right arm will straighten and revert back to its original address position at impact.

FUNCTION 2: ALLOWS CORRECT LEFT FOREARM ROTATION

It is almost impossible to create a good swing plane and to keep the clubface in a neutral position if your left arm does not initiate the correct movement in the takeaway. If your left elbow joint points to the left of your left hip at address, your left forearm will assume an over-rotated position, potentially leading to either an excessively flat backswing plane or a shut clubface in the takeaway.

Keeping the pockets of each inner elbow pointing outwards places your forearms in a neutral position and maximizes your chances of swinging on the correct plane.

POINT YOUR ELBOWS AT THEIR CORRESPONDING HIP JOINTS.

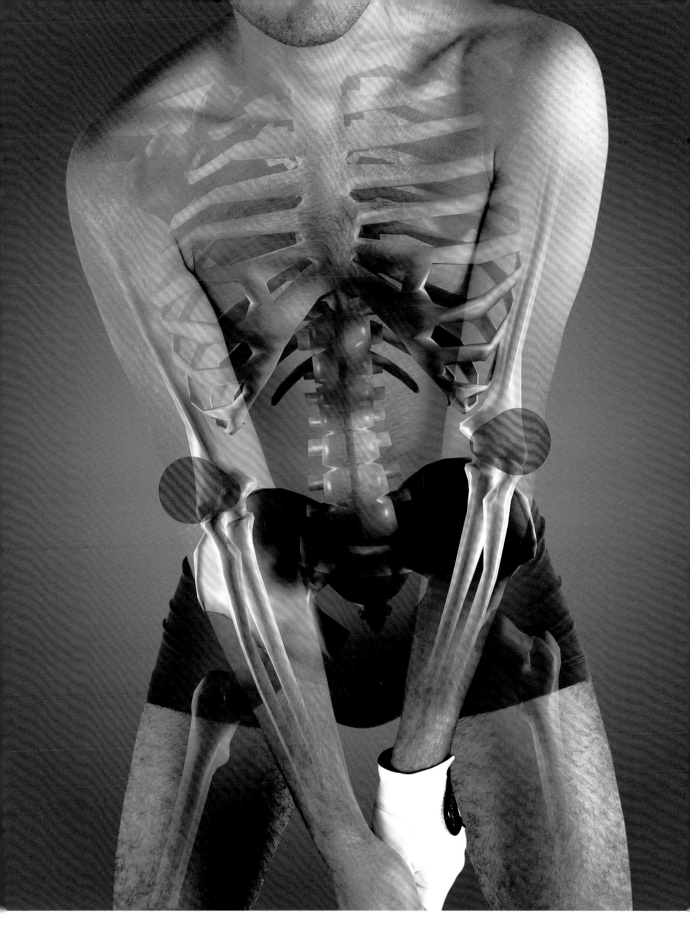

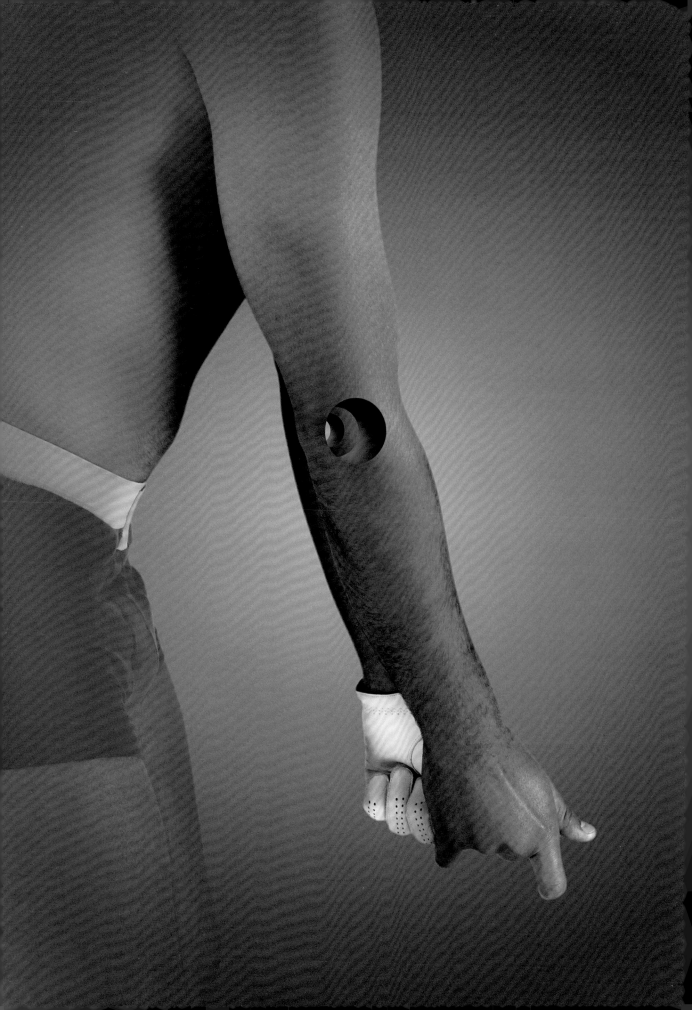

ARM ALIGNMENT—A SMALL DETAIL WITH BIG CONSEQUENCES

As the sternum moves from the sweeping position required to hit a driver to create the compressive angle required for hitting shorter irons, pitching and chipping, the positioning of your arms changes slightly. For example, when the sternum is angled backwards in order to sweep the ball off the tee with a driver or a long iron, your forearms should be square to each other and the target line. However, when you set up with the sternum slightly ahead of the ball to produce the steeper downward blow required to hit a pitch shot, for example, your right forearm will naturally be set noticeably higher than the left, while the alignment of your forearms will be slightly left of target.

SUMMARY—BUILD YOUR SWING FROM THE GROUND UPWARDS

The purpose of Law 2 is primarily to provide the golf swing with two important functions. Firstly, it allows your body, when positioned at address, to effectively punch in the coordinates for the type of strike and shot you wish to play. Secondly, it will enable you to position your body in its most efficient and powerful state in anticipation of the burst of motion that it is going to be created.

The information provided within this chapter can also serve as a detailed graphic menu for injury prevention. The waiting rooms of osteopaths, physiotherapists and chiropractors the world over are filled with amateur and professional golfers suffering with back ailments.

Another key focus of this chapter is that you must first look to the ground in your quest for consistency. Any golfer who focuses purely on refining the upper half of the body to the point of perfection, but disregards the role of the legs is destined for a lifetime of frustrating golf. However, the golfer who builds his or her swing from the ground upwards will always have a stable base upon which they can create a good shoulder turn or coil behind the ball. If you are in any doubt as to your swing priorities, refer to the "road map" of the swing on page 32.

Finally, always remember that the purpose of the set-up is to provide a balance between discipline and mobility that will stand you in good stead for the rest of the swing and set you on your way to learning how the legs and torso move in Law 3—Groundforce Dynamics.

◀ A DEPICTION OF STANDARD ARM ALIGNMENT AT ADDRESS.

LAW 3

GROUNDFORCE DYNAMICS
Creating a legendary leg action

INTRODUCTION

It is my prediction that during the years to come the role of the legs and the torso will, in addition to the grip, become the central focus of the golf swing. Athletic legwork facilitates and encourages good upper-body movement. The lower body, in conjunction with the torso, generates torque and coil in the golf swing—but this powerful movement can only be achieved when the body enjoys a stable relationship with the ground.

An analogy for good leg action can be found in the relationship between a bow and an arrow. As the arrow (the golf club) is drawn back, the wire (the arms and body) becomes stretched and taut as it moves further away from the bow (the ground), which remains in a fixed position. It would be impossible to create tension and power in the wire and an accurate flight of the arrow, if the bow was allowed to move around freely. While there is plenty of movement and motion in creating power, it has to be done with a link to stability.

Next to the grip, the role of the legs and the mid-section of the body is the second key fundamental of the swing that you must master.

Countless amateur golfers fail to find that happy medium between too little movement and too much. If there is too little movement, the upper body coil and wind never gets started. The player will then invariably get stuck over the ball in a reverse pivot scenario, where the weight remains on the front foot during the backswing. On the other hand, a golfer who is guilty of over-turning introduces so much movement into their swing that any hope of good timing and solid ball-striking fly out of the window.

If the average amateur golfer were to adopt the address position of a good Tour professional, probably the biggest difference they would notice would be the degree of knee flex. It would feel "squatty" and "alive" for the one simple reason that the closer you move your body to the ground while maintaining a good posture, the more potential power you have at your disposal.

The benefits of a strong mid-section and base are apparent to thousands of people who, each day, indulge in the increasingly popular exercise regimes of yoga and pilates, both of which focus on strengthening the body from within. This so-called "core" stability training is now wholly accepted by personal trainers, osteopaths and chiropractors alike and is also found in the best golf swings. If you can plant your center of gravity in the set-up position in such a way that it facilitates both torque and balance, a vital ingredient has been introduced to the swing.

This vital effect of the mid-section and the legs during the swing can be thought of rather like the ripples created when throwing pebbles into a pond. The shape of the first ripple will dictate the ripples that follow. When a pattern of motion, correct or incorrect occurs from the body's center, it will radiate outwards into the knees, hips, shoulders and ultimately the clubhead.

The theme of Law 3 is the relationship between the ground and the movement of the body. You will learn how to use your legs and the mid-section of your body to stack the body and "load" power correctly, allowing you to create maximum torque and resistance on the backswing and maximum power at impact.

LEARNING LEG ACTION FROM OTHER SPORTS

My experience in coaching players of all levels has taught me that some of the best analogies and examples of the correct leg action required in the golf swing can be found in other sports:

THE LEGS AT ADDRESS
Tennis—lively anticipation of the motion to come

The next time you watch a tennis tournament on television, pay particular attention to the players receiving serve. In a similar way to a cat poising its body before preparing to pounce, the tennis pros will shuffle around on the spot as they prepare themselves to react to the incoming ball and the dynamic move that they are about to make.

A golfer standing over the ball is clearly not able to make the same amount of movement as the tennis player, but the sensation of readiness should be almost identical. Many top golfers look as though they are gently crushing grapes under their feet as they get comfortable at address and prepare their body for the athletic movement to follow. The body searches for balance, energy and assistance from the ground as it secures its final footing before starting the swing motion.

Many amateur golfers would be well advised to imitate the body language of the tennis player. The golf swing does not work well from a "dead start." It needs a motion trigger to start the swing and it needs a rhythm to repeat that motion. While some of this can be supplied by the legs at address, the rest is created by the club and the hands.

THE LEGS IN THE BACKSWING
High diving—compress the legs against the ground to create power

The high diver and the golfer share a common goal—they both have to generate a great deal of power from the surface on which they stand. The high diver compresses himself onto the board using his body like a concertina to generate the power required to propel his body high into the air and away from the board. The legs and torso of the golfer act in a similar manner during the backswing. As the upper body and club move back, the legs should become progressively tighter until pure recoil sends the golfer into his downswing.

Later in this chapter, I will explain how controlling the motion of the torso is a fundamental requirement of a consistent and orthodox golf swing. As the "middle ground" of the swing, the way in which your torso behaves during the swing will determine to a large degree the roles played by the knees and the shoulders.

This middle ground is also crucial for the high diver. Without stacking his knees, hips and shoulders on top of one another like a three-story block of apartments as he lowers his body in readiness, he has no hope of exerting maximum power into his launch. The same is true of the impact position in golf. Maximum power and delivery can only be achieved through the perfect alignment of the major joints, thereby ensuring that the body's center of gravity is fully involved in the hit.

THE LEGS IN THE DOWNSWING
Boxing—delivering the knockout punch

Once torque, resistance and power have been created in the backswing, this energy must be transmitted into an effective force. Boxers and golfers need this focused energy as they home in on their respective targets. For the golfer, the target is the ball, while for the boxer it is whichever part of his opponent's body he is trying to hit.

The common denominator is the way in which both the boxer and the golfer use both sides of their body as they make their strike. As the fighter prepares to hit his opponent, he will draw his right side back, shift his weight and stretch away from his left side. This movement is mirrored in the best golf swings. The coil to the top of the backswing requires the left side of the body to resist the turning motion of the right. This in turn will stretch and tighten the body to a degree at which the downswing becomes an instinctive and uninhibited reaction.

The coil to the top of the back-swing requires the left side of the body to resist the turning motion of the right.

As the boxer moves forward to strike his opponent, he will plant his weight firmly on his left leg, creating a pillar against which he can slam the right side of his body as he unleashes his punch. When viewed in slow motion, this movement from the right side of the body to the left is a fluent, wave-like motion. First the weight transfers, moving the entire left side of the body over the supporting left leg, then the right side uses this support to deliver a blow using the whole of the torso. A boxer could never deliver a knockout punch by keeping his weight on his right side and flicking his wrist at his opponent's face.

PAST AND PRESENT EXAMPLES OF GREAT LEG ACTION

The best golf swings are founded upon solid and athletic leg action. What is the point of trying to cultivate the swing plane of a Ben Hogan or a Nick Faldo if your leg action is varied and inconsistent? When building your swing, you must always work from the ground upward.

There have been many wonderful examples of great lower-body action over the years. Copying Sam Snead's or Moe Norman's leg action would give a sensation of stability and consistency to any golfer's downswing. When observing Ben Hogan in action, you can see the fluidity and energy that made this small man's swing so explosive as he ripped through each and every shot.

In the modern era, the benefits of a stable backswing leg action are evident in the swing of the South African, Ernie Els. As he winds back deceptively slowly, he accumulates a tremendous torque, coil and power. However, I must say that the "pull hook" shot that Ernie occasionally experiences under pressure would disappear if he replicated Snead's "settled" downswing motion.

In firing the right side through the ball, you need look no further than Tiger Woods. As his swing switches gear, Woods fires the right side of his body into the ball with complete conviction. Long hitters must carry their right side all the way through to the end of the swing if their distance is to be accompanied by accuracy. Trevor Immelman of South Africa and England's David Howell are two other good, modern-day examples to look out for.

BALANCE—START AS YOU MEAN TO GO ON

Although the acid test of a golfer's balance takes place during the golf swing, it is important to realize that good balance should be present right from the outset at address. The triangular aspect of the stance outlined in Law 2 is the first key to achieving this.

When the middle of each foot is placed just outside the width of your hips, it allows your hips to rotate within the boundary formed by this position. However, if your stance is too narrow in relation to the hips, there is always a risk that the heavy mass of the torso will tilt and protrude outside of the stance, thus ruining the stability of the swing.

Good balance should be present right from the outset at address.

Another word for balance is equilibrium. Once you distribute the weight evenly between the left and right feet and between the heel and the toe, you have an equality of balance from which the swing can start its motion. From this point on, it will be the quality of the body motion that will either maintain or destroy any balance previously created.

THE RIGHT LEG—CREATING A BOUNDARY OF RESISTANCE IN THE BACKSWING

The more you can get right in the address position, the better chance you have of making a great swing. The role of the right leg during the backswing is one key element of the golf swing that you MUST get right. It not only serves as a power source, it also reduces the risk of poor body motion ruining your technique.

When examining the role of the right leg during the backswing, a good analogy is that of a battery waiting to be charged. At address you should feel lively and ready to go, while during the backswing, you should feel that the right leg increases its pressure into the ground. The more pressure you can "load" onto your right leg at this time, the more power you will have to offer the ball when you hit it.

PRACTICE EXERCISE: THE RIGHT LEG DRILL

The purpose of this exercise is simply to prevent the right side of the body from turning too much in the backswing. This is a fault that afflicts countless amateurs and professionals, and failing to temper an early turning motion of the body leads to poor positioning of the club and a lack of power.

The good news is that as soon as you perform this drill, you will immediately know whether you have been using your right side correctly during the backswing or not. In effect, your right knee is creating a boundary that you can load and coil into, but not beyond.

- Take your regular address position using a mid-iron and draw your left foot back until your big toe is in line with the heel of your right foot. Make sure that your stance is slightly narrower than normal and that the ball is about an inch inside your left heel.

- As you make your backswing, try to maintain the same amount of flex in your right knee that you introduced at address. Repeat this exercise until you can recreate the same feelings and positions in your real swing.

- One point worth noting is that this is a practice exercise designed to introduce the correct swing feelings. Although you can hit shots while performing the drill, striking the ball crisply and cleanly is not your main objective. Good ball-striking is an added bonus, not an essential.

It is impossible to create torque and resistance in your swing without stretching your muscles. This is why the legs play such a pivotal role in the creation of power. Using the ground as a firm base, you can "spring load" your body during the backswing. You can also create torque or coil in an athletic action when you use one side of the body to wind, or support the wind of another.

Many golfers focus primarily on their right leg during the backswing and pretty much dismiss the notion that the left leg plays a role of any importance in the backswing. However, it is the stretching away from the left side into the right side that allows the body to wind and coil on the backswing. If your left knee collapses and buckles in towards the right leg on the backswing, you are robbing your swing of vital resistance and power.

PRACTICE EXERCISE: THE LEFT LEG DRILL

This exercise is designed to add extra resistance to the left leg during the backswing.

- Address the ball normally, but turn your left foot outwards so that it points to between 9 and 10 on an imaginary clock face.

- Using a mid- to short-iron, make a couple of smooth and slow back swings. Remember that this is a stretching exercise and it is important that you should perform the drill slowly while you get used to the extra strain placed on your left leg. You will find that the left side of your body will experience a stretching sensation and feel as though it wants to recoil back into the ball.

- Always remember that during the backswing it is the turning of the torso that pulls the legs into position to create the stretch. Stretch slowly to the top and then smoothly down—two great keys for a well-timed golf swing.

THE 7 LAWS OF THE GOLF SWING

PRACTICE EXERCISE: SQUAT HITS—THE ULTIMATE DRILL FOR GREAT LEGWORK

To experience the way in which your legs should feel and behave in a great backswing try some squat hits. They will help you generate maximum torque in the golf swing and give your legs a really good workout at the same time. Ideally, you should perform this exercise regularly to ensure that your legs are working to their full capacity. In a standard one-hour practice session, you should hit at least 15 balls using this exercise.

• Assume your normal stance at address and then increase your knee flex by about 50 percent. As you do this, make sure that you maintain the two key posture curves that I discussed in Law 2 (page 39). The feeling you are looking for here is that of a weight-lifter squatting in preparation to snatch the bar upwards. As you have lowered your body considerably, it is advisable to use a club with a slightly flatter lie angle—a 6-iron or 5-iron, for example, rather than a pitching wedge.

- In addition to encouraging a good coil and wind on the backswing, squat hits also train the body to maintain a low center of gravity through impact and beyond. This is particularly beneficial during the change of direction between backswing and downswing where all of the body planes flatten a little. This concept will be explained in more detail during Law 5, but, for the time being, simply be aware of the reduction in the movement of the lower body allied to a tighter and more effective coil.

- By squatting at address you have effectively preset some of that essential coil. Remember that the body gains a large degree of its power by "scrunching" itself into the ground. This whole drill is based on the principles outlined in Law 2, which refer to the use of the ground during the entire swing. The ground is the only truly solid platform that you can rely on to create balance, consistency and power, and this drill gives you a glimpse of this key relationship by moving you closer to it.

- I recommend that you tee the ball up when hitting shots using this drill. Make a smooth, full wind on the backswing and clip the ball away. If your leg action has previously been weak and slack, this drill will give you an immediate sensation of compression and tightness together with a new feeling of acceleration into the ball.

STACKING THE DRUM ALLOWS BODY TO TURN, NOT TILT

If you can move your belt in a purely rotational fashion during the swing you have won golf's equivalent of the lottery! What you actually see in the following images is not just the level rotation of the belt during the swing, but the blending of three major joints—the shoulders, hips and knees.

If the mid-section of your body moves correctly in the rotational fashion shown, these key body parts stack up nicely on top of one another and place the center of the body in the ideal position to deliver the club into the ball.

You may find it useful to imagine an oil drum that has been cut into three pieces as in this torso key image. The top segment represents the shoulders, the middle represents the torso, and the bottom section is the knees. If you knocked out the middle piece, the other two would simply collapse. When the hips tilt during the swing, extreme pressure is placed on the body, forcing it to compensate with excessive hand action through the ball.

Structurally, this is also bad news for the spine and the knees, since tilting your hips places extreme pressure on the other body joints and the spine. Your body wants to move in a rotational manner, since this is how it was designed. If your left hip tilts downwards during the backswing and your right hip tilts downwards in the downswing in a misguided attempt to get the ball into the air, your body will be prevented from turning and working with optimum efficiency.

However, if you can keep all three sections of the drum stacked on top of each other it is much easier to achieve a great backswing, impact and follow-through. When the belt and mid-section rotate correctly during the backswing, the shoulders can turn and wind a full 90 degrees without any hindrance or strain.

THIS BARREL IMAGE DEPICTS THE CORRECT
STACKING OF THE BODY'S MAJOR JOINTS.

LEVEL BELT LINE KEEPS STERNUM
IN OPTIMUM IMPACT POSITION

From a ball-striking perspective, keeping your belt line level throughout the swing enables your sternum—or chest bone—to return to the optimum position at impact and prevents it from being thrown backwards, which would move the low point of the swing too far behind the ball. When it comes to creating power, it is far better to have all of your weight moving towards the target than

▼ IF YOU LEARN TO KEEP YOUR BELT LINE LEVEL, YOUR SWING WILL BENEFIT.

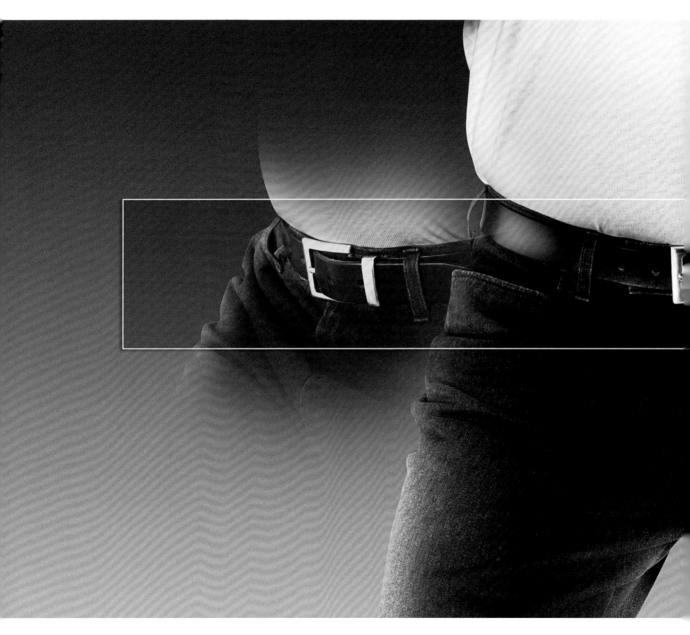

just a small proportion of it. If your hips tilt and thrust forwards in the downswing while your body weight is either static or falling away from the target, you can almost guarantee poor striking and power.

Ask yourself one simple question: If you want to push a car 20 yards down the road, would it be easier if you pushed it only with your hips or the whole of your body? Rehearse the motion illustrated below as regularly as possible in front of a mirror, ensuring that any hip tilt is kept to an absolute minimum.

HOW TILTING HIPS CAN AFFECT YOUR HITS

Even a non-golfer or complete beginner would know instinctively that there is something drastically wrong with the golf swing demonstrated below. With such an ungainly technique, it is clear that the golfer is going to struggle to hit the ball crisply and powerfully. After errors in the grip, tilting the hips is the golf swing's public enemy number one.

Image 1: It is evident here that somebody has kicked out the middle section of that oil drum mentioned earlier. Instead of turning away from the target, the golfer here has simply rocked his shoulders and tilted his hips.

IMAGE 1 (LEFT) AND IMAGE 2 (RIGHT): BUSTING OUTSIDE
THE BOUNDARIES OF THE GOLF SWING.

Image 2: When the hips tilt again in the downswing, the sternum and breastbone are forced away from the target into a position where they are way behind the ideal ball-striking point. This golfer has had no alternative but to compensate for the poor body motion with excessive hand action. As the sternum moves back, the hands have to move unnaturally forward.

Both images show how the relationship between the shoulders, hips and knees has deteriorated. They have become so fragmented, disjointed and independent that there is only one result: a powerless and disorganized lunge into the ball that makes it almost impossible to squeeze the ball into the turf.

"TILTING" IS THE REMOVAL OF THE MID-SECTION OF THE BARREL,
PRODUCING AN UNSTABLE AND INCONSISTENT MOTION.

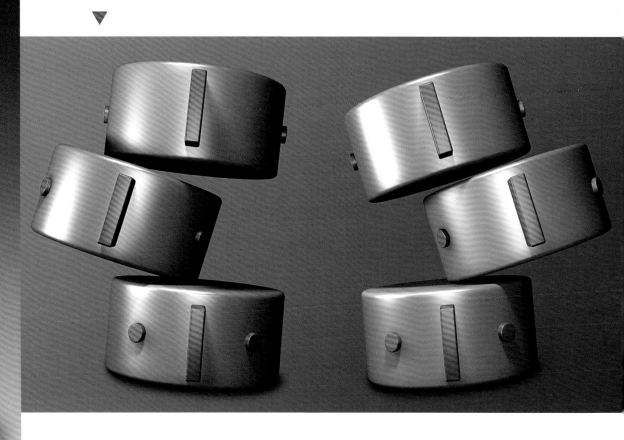

HOW YOUR MID-SECTION HOLDS ORBIT

In Law 2, I introduced you to the concept of the all-important "middle ground of your swing." With the exception of the grip, this central area of your body is the catalyst of almost all of the motion that will take place during the swing. There are three reasons why it has this authority and responsibility:

- Your balance is controlled from an area just below the sternum.
- The quality of the torso motion determines the movement of the shoulders and knees.
- The torso is the swing's center of gravity.

Once the correct address position has been adopted, certain aspects of your body are strategically placed to play crucial roles within the swing. When your mid-section moves correctly—or

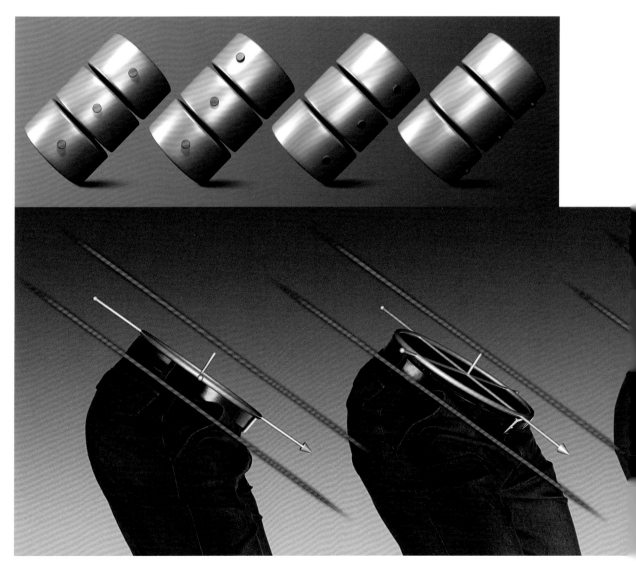

indeed incorrectly—a ripple effect takes place that spreads towards the rest of your swing. The images below portray the exact motion that is required from the trunk to enable the swing to find its most efficient route back and through the ball.

As you can see, the belt line and inclination remain exactly the same throughout the whole motion. This ensures that everything revolving around the mid-section remains in the same "orbit." The reason why the belt or trouser line is such a great reference point for this particular aspect of the swing is because it is located directly above the hip joints, which are the main focus of attention. In addition to the belt line maintaining its position, look at the angles formed by the lower back, rump and thighs. These also maintain their start-up positions perfectly during the swing. Although they are only able to do this when the torso moves correctly and consistently, their positioning can still be used as a valuable reference.

Looking at the swing from the "down the line" perspective (overleaf), you can really appreciate the almost dictatorial effect that the mid-section and legs have on the upper body. Without stability and consistency of movement from the lower body, the upper body will struggle to perform well.

Whatever degree of inclination the belt assumes at address must be maintained throughout the swing motion. Practice this regularly—it is a very important fundamental of the golf swing.

THE IMAGE BELOW AND THE BARREL REPRESENTATION (LEFT)
DEPICT THE MID-SECTION HOLDING ITS ORBIT.

UPPER TORSO MOTION IS SUPPORTED BY LOWER TORSO MOTION.

Life becomes considerably easier for the golf swing when the legs and trunk are used efficiently and correctly. If the mid-section of your body rotates in a cylindrical fashion, your shoulders will instinctively pitch and turn in the correct manner. This is what the role of the legs is all about: they instigate the correct motion from the torso and then support it when this happens.

In Law 2, I explained that the spine tilts slightly away from the target at address. This small move away from the perpendicular produces many benefits, one of which is that it negates the need to consciously transfer the weight in the backswing. In actual fact, the weight transference required in a good golf swing is far less than most people imagine.

Any movement on the backswing has to be replaced and increased slightly in order to achieve a great impact position. So if you over-turn on your backswing and shift your weight substantially, you place a huge demand on the downswing in order to return the club to the ball correctly.

Once the subtle spine angle tilt is installed at address, you no longer need to consciously think about shifting your weight. Simply coiling your shoulders around the axis of the spine will automatically create all the weight transfer that you need.

Assuming that your basics are orthodox, the only way that you can fail to transfer your weight correctly is if you allow your mid-section to tilt, forcing the right hip into a high position where it obstructs the trunk from rotating. The two images here highlight the two crucial moves that you need to install and maintain into your upper torso pivot.

Image 1
From the "face-on" angle, you can see how the hips have rotated on a nice level plane and the knees and legs look tight and disciplined. All of the correct ingredients to fuel a great body pivot are visible, including the effects of the slight rearward tilt of the spine (Torque 1).

While the hips have rotated on a fairly single plane, the upper body has subtly angled itself away from the target. You will find, however, that the head will still want to swivel back to a position where it looks directly down at the ball in the six o'clock position (Torque 2). This is perfectly acceptable and vital in order to maximize the backswing coil. However, do not let the head turn more than this. If your head swivels into a position where it looks down to the left of the ball, you are encouraging a reverse pivot and, with it, a powerless golf swing.

Finally, it is important to discuss the amount of turn that the key components of the body achieve within a good pivot motion. In an ideal world, the shoulders wind to about 90 degrees as the hips turn about 45 degrees on completion of the backswing. However, it is important to realize that, over the years, many top players have produced great golf with significantly more or less turn than this.

If you are particularly flexible, you may benefit from a bigger upper-body coil. It is also possible to play great golf if your body frame is tight and features little in the way of flexibility. In both instances, though, it is crucial that you maintain the synchronization of the clubhead in relation to the speed of the body. In Law 4 we will look at this aspect of the swing in more detail.

Image 2

The "down the line" view on page 72 highlights the effects of geometry rather than abundant power. The angle of the spine created at address has been maintained all the way to the top. This occurs when the left shoulder is allowed to pitch downward slightly from its starting position during the backswing. Another key feature of the set-up that has not changed in the slightest is the position of the right knee. Although it has partially rotated in response to the movement of the trunk, it has still pretty much held its original start-up angle. The left knee here has also shown good discipline.

The upper body and torso control the movement of the left knee during the backswing. The coiling of the upper body pulls the left knee slightly inward towards the ball so that the weight transfers to the instep of the left foot. The only voluntary and conscious movement permissible from the legs occurs with the right leg and knee during the downswing, which I will explain in more detail in Law 6. Anything else is inefficient and wasted motion.

Finally, it is important to highlight the fact that there is no visible gap between the legs from this angle. This illustrates that they are supporting and controlling the upper body. If they were to have assumed a "scissor legs" position, where a window of light can be seen between the legs, it is likely that the upper body would have over-turned or reverse pivoted.

SUMMARY

Law 2 is capable of turning a golfer who looks weak and fragile standing over the ball into a person who is grounded and strong at address. In fact, "grounded" and "strong" are the keywords for any structure that seeks stability above the ground.

This concept does not stop at address however. The good work carried out in the previous chapter must be continued within the swing motion. Law 3 has shown how to maximize the power that you possess in your legs and trunk. The right and left leg drills enable you to create and recognize the stretching sensation that is needed to "wind" the lower body against its closest ally, the ground.

This chapter has also shown that the swing motion must be disciplined. The key lesson is that the upper body, belt line and mid-section move in a rotational, not a tilted fashion and, in doing so, are capable of pivoting correctly around the spine throughout the swing. This is a prerequisite for pure ball-striking and easy power.

To a large degree, a golfer with good legwork during the backswing will invariably have good legwork in the downswing and, in Law 6, I will examine in more detail the vital role that the legs play in the downswing and through impact. For the time being, however, there is no finer exercise than "squat hits" to create the correct sensations in your legs during the backswing. This exercise keeps the center of gravity low throughout the swing, thereby maximizing your ability to wind and create pressure, and also serves to discipline and shorten any unruly arm swing.

As the rate of motion now present in the golf swing begins to increase, your next step is to learn how to blend the movement of the golf club and the arm swing into the turning of the body in Law 4—Synchronicity: The swing's dimension of time.

LAW 4

SYNCHRONICITY
The swing's dimension of time

INTRODUCTION

It would be great if you could pinpoint the very essence of great timing in the golf swing. However, while improved coaching methods and technologies over the past decade or so have allowed us to achieve a far better understanding of what constitutes good swing technique, one factor that remains elusive to many golfers is good timing. While this does not usually present a problem for most top players, it often remains tantalizingly out of reach for the average amateur golfer.

The modern golf swing demonstrated by many leading Tour professionals is becoming increasingly uniform. This is to be expected as it is simply a reflection of a general standardization of coaching beliefs and methods combined with an increased awareness of subjects such as sports science and biomechanics.

One factor that remains elusive to many golfers is good timing.

The culmination of this enhanced knowledge is the development of a more efficient, powerful and manageable swing motion, and this makes it much easier to track down the rogue elements of the swing that can lead to poor timing. In the past, searching for the causes of poor timing and tempo was like looking for a needle in a haystack. Now, however, once you have recognized your fault you can simply refer to the images and practice drills in this chapter to rectify the problem.

In order to gain a clearer understanding of the timings involved in the golf swing, it is important that you become aware of the "big picture." The most important relationship discussed in this chapter is that between the clubhead, the arms and the body. In years gone by, I believe there has been an overemphasis on moving everything together at one speed. As you will see, if this is over done, however good the intention may be, it will upset the individual timings of the swing motion.

DISTANCES, SPEEDS AND DIRECTIONS

If all of the moving parts in your swing traveled exactly the same distance and at the same speed, golf would be much easier to master. It would simply be a case of everything starting and finishing together. Unfortunately, the reality is completely different. The distance traveled by the clubhead during the average golf swing is in excess of 10 feet, while the torso's journey can be measured in inches. Therefore, in order to create a golf swing that starts and finishes together, some parts of the body and the club must travel more quickly than others.

The rhythm of your swing plays a key role in ensuring that the various moving parts in your swing remain synchronized. For example, if the golf club and the body have the same rhythm and motion during the early stages of the backswing, the larger muscles of the torso will dominate the backswing and drag the hands, arms and clubhead too far inside the desired swing plane. The swing synchronicity chart below will help you gain a clearer understanding of this concept.

THE SWING SYNCHRONICITY CHART

Starting from the ground, the golf swing becomes progressively faster as you move upwards. The ground is still, as it has nowhere to go. Your feet move the smallest distance at the slowest speed, while the clubhead has to move the fastest simply because it has the longest distance to travel. Your goal is to blend these individual timings into one perfectly synchronized whole.

You may find it useful to think of the relationship between the body and the clubhead as similar to that of the hub and perimeter of a wheel. While the inner hub rotates in a small circle, the outer rim of the wheel travels at a much greater speed to cover the extra distance. The golf swing works in exactly the same way.

THE SWING SYNCHRONICITY CHART. ▶

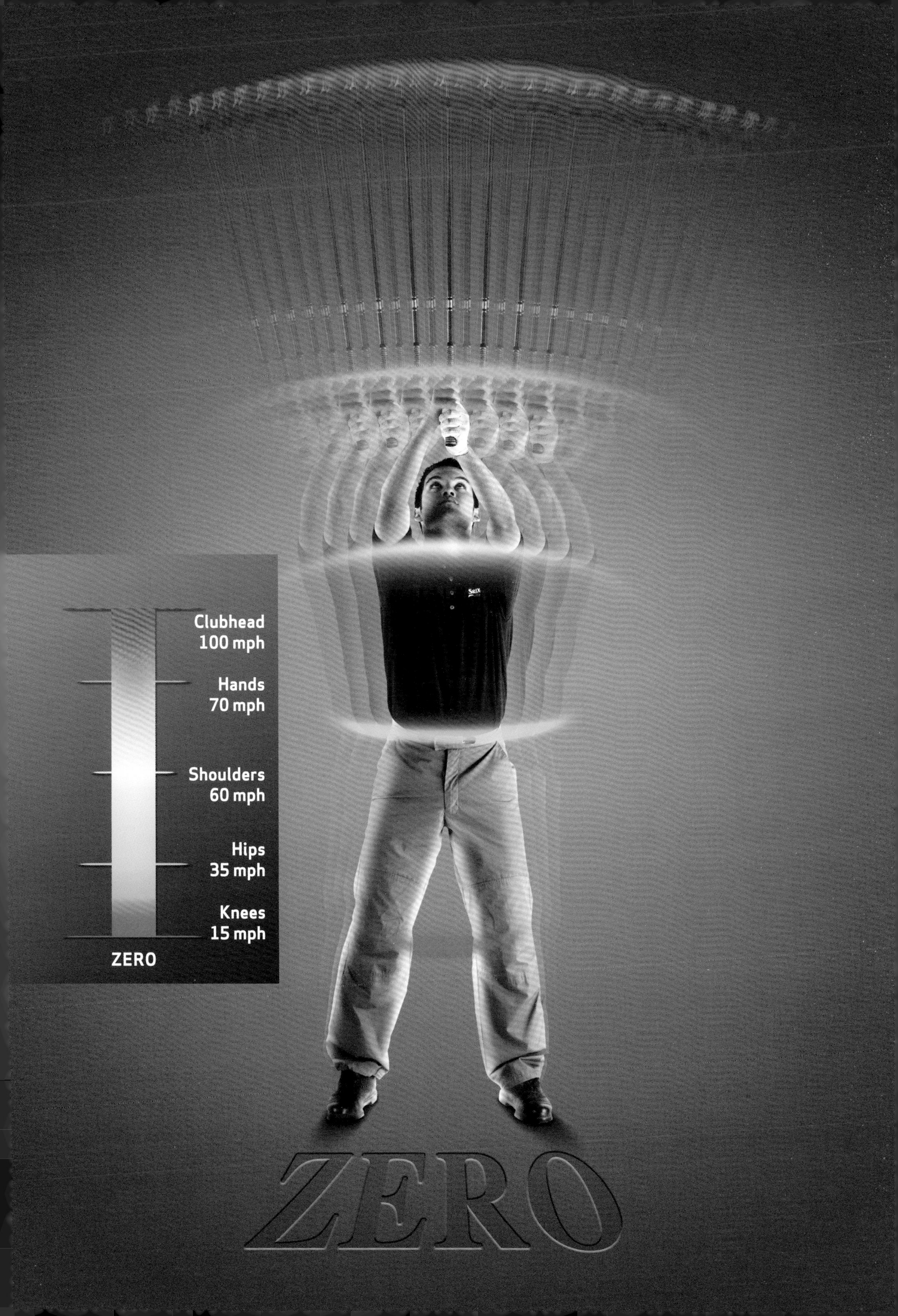

Clubhead
100 mph

Hands
70 mph

Shoulders
60 mph

Hips
35 mph

Knees
15 mph

ZERO

ZERO

RHYTHM AND BEAT—BRING YOUR SWING SPEED RATIOS CLOSER TOGETHER

The rhythm displayed in a Tour professional's powerful and efficient golf swings will always have a fairly two-beat nature—by this I mean that the speeds of the backswing and downswing are fairly similar. In direct contrast, the difference between the backswing and downswing speeds of the average club golfer can often be poles apart.

The golfer who swings back at, say, 20 mph has no other option than to sling his or her body into the shot at 80 mph to generate the power necessary to hit the ball a significant distance. The disparity in speed between backswing and downswing will invariably destroy your timing and control over the ball.

Similarly, if your backswing is an 80 mph blur of motion, you will have no alternative but to ease up to something around 20 mph through the ball in order to achieve some degree of control over the shot. The great players realize the importance of building and maintaining swing momentum.

RHYTHM AND TEMPO

While the tempo of a swing can change from player to player, good rhythm must be fairly uniform. The tempo of your swing is usually governed and dictated by your temperament and personality. If you have a fast, upbeat personality, you will struggle to slow your swing down with any great permanency. Similarly, naturally slower swingers who try to inject more speed into their swing in an attempt to hit the ball further will also face problems. In order to improve, both types of golfer will have to work with the tempo that they naturally possess and resolve to create a fluent rhythm through improved swing mechanics.

Two players who typify the difference between rhythm and tempo are Ernie Els and Nick Price. The laid-back, lumbering and large-framed Ernie Els will always possess a slower tempo than that of Nick Price, who walks and talks quickly; however, both players possess a good two-beat swing ratio.

◀ IT IS IMPORTANT TO GAIN A CLEAR UNDERSTANDING OF THE TIMINGS INVOLVED IN THE GOLF SWING.

TORQUE 2—HEAD TURNS TO FACE THE BALL AT THE TOP

You were introduced to Torque 1 during Law 2. As you may remember, it serves three important purposes. It aligns the spine from top to bottom, it negates the need for a conscious weight transfer on the backswing and it prevents the upper body from turning too quickly and disrupting the timing of the whole swing. However, when the time comes for your body to turn, your head will have to swivel to allow your shoulders to rotate fully. Torque 2 focuses purely on creating the correct degree of head turn.

If your head is allowed to turn too much during the backswing, all sense of coil and torque is lost, resulting in a slack and lifeless swing and a loss of power and authority at impact. An over-rotation of the head also disrupts the synchronicity of the swing. When very little resistance is created, your arms have a free rein during the backswing and will tend to travel too far in relation to the turning of the shoulders.

When the body is wound and tight at the top of the backswing, it is in its optimum position.

Torque 2 allows the head to turn just a little so that it is directly facing at the ball at the top of the backswing. Limiting the head motion stretches and winds the upper back muscles in an efficient manner. When the body is wound and tight at the top of the backswing it is in its optimum position, but this desirable feeling is not something that you should just stumble upon. It will help you achieve a compact yet powerful top of the backswing in a quick, efficient and consistent manner.

TORQUE 2—LIMIT HEAD MOTION TO WIND THE
UPPER BACK MUSCLES EFFICIENTLY. ▶

As I mentioned in Law 2, it is vital that your body does not turn too early in the backswing, otherwise the timing of your swing and the positioning of the club can be severely disrupted. During the early stages of the backswing, the club must enjoy an initial independence from the body—a head start—if it is to move away on the correct path and plane. As you will discover in the next chapter, there is an optimum swing plane that delivers guaranteed consistency and simplicity, but this can only be achieved if the first stage of your backswing is well timed.

As gruesome as this image may seem, it is an accurate portrayal of the correct timing sequence. The spear completely stifles the body's attempt to turn, enabling the golfer to set the club on the correct plane. From this position, the torso now coils around the angle of the spine and winds the arms up to the top of the backswing. Before you can do this, however, it is essential that you have the right imagery and feeling in your mind when meshing your arms and your body together during the golf swing.

PRACTICE EXERCISE:
THE SEQUENCING DRILL

- Assume a potent address position. Now close your eyes and picture a spear entering your back, running through to your navel and into the ground.

- Keeping your hands relatively low and in front of your body, move the club into its mid-plane position (turn to page 108 for details).

- The final part of the drill is to snap the spear by allowing the torso to play its role and coil against the resistance of the lower body to create a correctly sequenced backswing.

- It is important to remember that this is only a practice drill. You should never consciously attempt to piece the backswing together in this fashion while on the golf course.

CLUB AND ARMS FIRST . . . THEN WIND THE BODY. ▶

PHYSIOLOGY OF THE ARMS

Your arms play a key role in the golf swing since they are the transmitters of power from your body to your hands, wrists and clubhead. They are also instrumental in determining the correct sequencing and timing of the backswing, so it is important to look in a little more detail at how they function.

THE LEFT ARM—RELAXED, NOT RIGID

One of the most common faults in the backswing stems from the belief that you must keep your left arm rigid and straight during the swing in order to create width, precision and power. Unfortunately, this normally has exactly the opposite effect. While it may feel powerful, attempting to keep your left arm as straight as possible as you sweep the club straight back away from the ball on a wide arc will actually limit the amount of power you can create in the swing.

The result of keeping your left arm rigid and tense is twofold. First, the clubhead will travel on an unnaturally wide arc on the backswing and probably cause the clubface to remain closed or hooded during the takeaway. During the change of direction between backswing and downswing, the forces exerted on your left arm will cause your wrists to flex excessively, leading to a narrow, steep arc that creates a whole array of ball-striking problems.

The second problem is that forcing your left arm to remain straight causes your body to turn too early in the backswing. If your upper-body coil is already complete when your arms have not even reached their halfway-back position, your arms will inevitably have to complete the rest of their journey to the top on their own, resulting in poor strikes and directional problems.

PRACTICE EXERCISE:
THE MOON CRESCENT DRILL

- Assume your normal address position, but remove your right hand from the club and place it in the fold of your left elbow. Keeping your right hand in this position, swing back with your left arm and allow it to bend slightly until you create the subtle "moon crescent" shape shown in this image.

- Once you have performed this exercise a few times, place your right hand back on the club and make some practice backswings, recreating the "soft and narrow" feeling. As soon as you are comfortable with this feeling, try hitting some practice balls while focusing on the new feeling of lightness in your left arm.

- When performing this drill, take note of the sensations that you experience. It will be a totally different feeling to the rigidity of your normal swing. Could you imagine trying to crack a whip while keeping your arms dead straight? Of course not! Your ability to create power would all but disappear. The same concept applies to the golf swing.

ALLOWING THE LEFT ARM TO BEND BREAKS
THE CIRCUIT OF TENSION

Allowing the left arm to bend a little on the backswing is perfectly acceptable, normal and, in fact, beneficial, since it breaks the circuit of tension that is created when your left arm remains locked out. The more relaxed muscles allow the arms to travel faster than the body, which encourages the correct synchronization with the turning motion of the torso.

As the swing arc and radius becomes a little more natural, you will sense that the arms and club also begin to feel much lighter. It is more than mere coincidence that if you make some one-handed practice swings, you instinctively find this natural arc.

SYNCHRONIZATION FAULT 1—CASTING THE CLUB, LOSING YOUR FEEL FOR THE CLUBHEAD

As we discussed in Law 1, the way in which you place your hands on the golf club directly influences the quality of your golf swing. However, it is not just the way in which you position your hands on the grip that determines your ability to create clubhead speed and power, but how much pressure you apply with them.

CASTING—THE PRODUCT OF A TIGHT HOLD.

Your subconscious mind continually monitors the position of the clubface during the swing. While you are probably blissfully unaware of this behind the scenes activity, this vital information is transmitted to your brain through your grip; firstly by its positioning and secondly by the amount of pressure applied. When you grip the club too tightly, you effectively shut off all communication between the clubhead and the brain. This restricts your ability to sense and feel the weight of the clubhead during the swing and, in turn, reduces your swing speed, power and accuracy of strike at impact.

This fault is referred to as "casting" because it resembles the action of casting a fishing rod. From the top of the backswing, the hands and arms force the club away from the body in an unnaturally wide arc. All leverage is lost when this happens. The arms, hands and wrists lose their elasticity and with it the ability to flex and increase the swinging weight of the golf club.

As the downswing progresses, the swing arc increases to the point where the clubhead is scooped upwards ahead of the hands. The resulting strike is almost always behind the ball. The other impact characteristic of a casting strike is the absence of compression into the back of the ball and the turf. No real divot is taken, just an untidy scuff in the ground way before the ball.

▲
THE BROKEN AND POORLY RELEASED LEFT FOREARM—A PRODUCT OF TENSION AND CASTING.

CURE—LET GO OF CONTROL . . . PLEASE!

The most common cause of casting is the overwhelming desire to control the golf club during the swing. It is interesting to note that those golfers most likely to suffer from this fault are those who exert a great deal of control over their private and professional lives. The feeling of relaxing, letting go and trusting the clubhead to do the work is as unnatural to them as letting external influences shape their destiny.

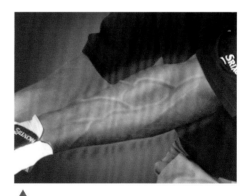

▲
TENSION IN THE LEFT-HAND GRIP AND FOREARM REDUCES THE SWINGING AND PULLING WEIGHT OF THE GOLF CLUB.

PRACTICE EXERCISE: THE WHIP DRILL

If you have grown accustomed to holding the club too tightly, this exercise is designed to help you restore your feel for the clubhead. It may cause your swing to feel a little out of control, but this liberation is very good for you.

This practice drill allows you to gain an enhanced awareness of the swinging weight of the club while allowing the momentum of the swing to create power, not brute strength. For optimum results, restrict yourself to making three-quarter-length swings so that you can get a better feel for the sensations involved.

Assume your normal address position and momentarily leave the clubhead behind the ball as your hands start the backswing. I refer to this as "undynamic lag." The momentum of the backswing will eventually move the clubhead away from the ball. Similarly, allow the club to lag behind the hands and idle behind the body-turn in the downswing by keeping your grip pressure nice and soft. You are now creating power through the forces of leverage or what I refer to as "dynamic lag."

LISTEN FOR THE PERFECT PITCH

It is important to remember that when you let go of control and give the club the freedom to revolve around your body, it will create a high-pitched swishing sound. When your grip pressure is too tight, it is impossible to create this sound in the downswing and instead you will create a low drone or, in many instances, no sound whatsoever. Make some practice swings without a ball and listen for the sound of your swing. If you are met with a wall of silence, it is time to lighten up!

SYNCHRONIZATION FAULT 2—NARROW, EXPLOSIVE AND UNCONTROLLABLE

There are occasions when the opposite of casting can arise. If your grip becomes too slack and your arms soften too much in the downswing, the radius of the downswing can become too narrow and lead to inconsistencies in divot patterns, distance control and trajectory. This type of downswing displays no discipline in the clubhead, especially in its delivery into the ball.

Instead of a release of power that is dispersed evenly through the impact area, the release of a narrow downswing is often explosive and violent. I liken this to jogging down a cliff pathway. Although you start off in full control, slowly but surely your speed will increase in response to the momentum of the slope until you burst into a frenzied sprint before falling over at the end. In this type of narrow swing, as the club, hands and arms progress through the impact area they often feel as though they are detached from the body and working in a completely different time zone.

The secret is to release your hands consistently throughout the downswing, not just at impact. If your hand action is absent in the early part of the downswing it is likely that your release at impact will be too explosive and uncontrolled.

NARROW, EXPLOSIVE AND POORLY TIMED.
▼

CURE—TREAT THE CLUB LIKE A FEATHER

The objective of the following drill is twofold. Firstly, it will encourage you to energize the shaft of the club so that it moves faster than the core of the body. Secondly, it will provide you with three vital timing reference points for the everyday maintenance of your swing. Starting from address, swing back until your wrists are fully set, release them at impact and then reset them in the follow-through. Throughout this series of movements, your goal is to make the club feel as light as a feather during the swing.

SET AND RESET. WORK THE CLUB LIKE THIS FEATHER.

PRACTICE EXERCISE: SET AND RESET

Select a mid- to short-iron and start making some small practice swings. As you do this, try to feel as though the clubhead is zipping around your body, which should remain fairly still and central. Once you become accustomed to the feelings, you can progress to hitting some shots off a tee peg and then on to striking the ball for real.

You will know when you are performing this exercise well when the following three things occur:

- Your divots become nice and shallow.

- You develop a more penetrating and powerful ball flight. The ball will fly a considerable distance considering that this is only really a hands and arms shot.

- Your swing will feel very neat from start to finish. It will start, wind and finish as one complete movement.

RECOIL—THE AFTER-EFFECT OF A FAST AND EFFICIENT ARM-SWING

If your swing is a little lackluster, recoiling the club back down in front of you may be the solution to your problems. One of the most obvious clues that your arms may be lagging too far behind your body in the downswing is the look and feel of your follow-through.

This type of follow-through often looks as though it is in slow motion compared to the rest of the body. The arms will give the impression of a downswing afterthought as they dawdle slowly into their follow-through position. This fault carries the penalty of poor strikes and inconsistent direction. Recoiling the club back in front of the body like this will iron out the problem by improving the coordination of your downswing.

THE RECOIL: BENEFIT 1

You will know when you recoil your club and arms correctly because they will literally bounce back in front of the body immediately upon completion of the follow-through. The immediate benefit of the recoil is the speed that it induces. A golf club that shows good speed will perform with greater efficiency than one that idles at a slow pace. Because a quicker-moving club will employ more inertia and momentum, its ability to "hold its course" becomes greatly assisted with more speed. Recoiling the club also endorses the basic statement of this Law, which is, "As the clubhead moves further than the body during the golf swing it must move faster to promote good synchronization between the two."

▲ THE RECOIL—THE PRODUCT OF A GREAT ARM SWING.

THE RECOIL: BENEFIT 2

The recoil can also provide a good indication of the quality of the body motion during the down-swing and into the follow-through. Your spine angle should remain on the constant incline that was created at address from start to finish and the recoiled finish position can highlight how well you have managed to achieve this.

As you work on your body motion, simply copy the second recoil image shown. After the ball has been struck, allow the club to drop back down in front of your body at the same angle as the spine. If it represents an angle of about 45 degrees, then the body has maintained its posture throughout the swing.

PRACTICE EXERCISE: TOTAL RECOIL

Start by ensuring that your grip features the "short left thumb" as discussed in Law 1 and that your grip pressure is uniform throughout. Waggle the clubhead with authority. As you do this, resist any movement with the body and keep the hands in front of your navel. Remember, you must encourage the clubhead to move faster than, and independently from, your body.

Start the swing with the same feeling gained with your waggle. As you reset the club on the downswing and into the follow-through, do so with such speed that the club "recoils" back in front of the body and back down in front of you.

SWING SYNCHRONICITY

The image overleaf provides an accurate blueprint of what you should be looking to achieve with the club and your body in a well-timed golf swing. It also provides you with a "time check" that enables you to measure the speed of your body and the clubhead. As with any aspect of the golf swing, I recommend that you always use a video camera when working on the finer points of your technique.

Starting with the golf club, in order to build a consistent and well-grooved golf swing, you will need key reference points. This image highlights one of these key points. What you see here is the club setting and resetting around the body in a totally symmetrical fashion. Pay particular attention to the shading of the body. You will see that the club has moved a considerable distance in relation to the torso, thus avoiding the killer fault of allowing the upper body to turn too soon.

◀ ONE BENEFIT OF THE RECOIL IS THAT IT PROVIDES
A VITAL SWING REFERENCE POINT.

SUMMARY

There is a distinct similarity between golf and dancing, in that if you don't know what happens and when, things can go horribly wrong! Fortunately, I have never subscribed to the belief that some people just don't have it. Good coordination is a skill that you can learn with practice, not just something that you are born with.

This is evidenced by good golfers who possess the most ungainly motion yet still manage to strike the ball sweetly time after time. So how do they do it? More often than not, the players have managed—undoubtedly with a little trial and error—to link the various moving parts of their body and the golf club extremely well through impact.

Players of all abilities are always looking for the perfect rhythm that will lead to great timing. Law 4 has provided you with the technical information to understand the "why" and the "when" of the golf swing. Rhythm is by and large your technical ability to mesh the various parts of the swing together smoothly. Tempo, on the other hand, is the speed at which you achieve this and is generally determined by your temperament and personality.

This book is designed to teach a low-maintenance swing. Golfers with poor technique and timing have to practice twice as much as those who have diligently created a good motion. If you regularly video your golf swing, you may notice slight changes in its shape after you have used the information in this chapter. Golfers who have struggled with certain positional problems will be surprised at the results they can achieve if they first consider the synchronicity of the swing before its shape. Assuming that the set-up is correct, over-zealous body motion is responsible for poor positioning of the club on both the backswing and the downswing in some 80 percent of cases.

So if you are one of those golfers who have been told or believe that you just don't have it, now is the time to reconsider. Good timing and coordination are factors that can be learned through trial and error and/or acquiring the correct information. As you develop the overall timing of your swing through Law 4 you will also start to create its shape, which leads perfectly to Law 5—Swing Plane: The most direct route from address to impact.

AN ILLUSTRATION OF GOOD SWING SYNCHRONICITY.

LAW 5

SWING PLANE
The most direct route from address to impact

INTRODUCTION

The subject of swing plane—what it should ideally be—has probably generated more debate among coaches and players than any other aspect of golf swing theory. However, achieving a good plane should be as straightforward as learning and maintaining any other key element of the swing motion.

Due to the infinite number of postures and positions that the human body can assume at address, the golf swing has many different guises. Combine this with the similarly infinite number of ways in which you can swing the club and you can begin to appreciate how the subject of plane can become clouded.

One of the main problems is that it is virtually impossible to visually monitor the plane and shape of your own swing unless you have access to a video camera. You might argue that this must be the same for almost every part of the swing, and to a certain extent you would be correct, but checking your own plane is particularly difficult because it involves keeping track of the fastest-moving aspect of the swing—the clubhead—which is swinging at speed around your body and out of your field of vision.

If I asked a selection of golfers to define and explain the term "swing plane," almost everybody would immediately refer to the positioning of the arms or the clubshaft during the swing. Very few would think to mention the influence of the body pivot, yet the coiling of the torso around the spine plays a funda-

The best players are aware of the vital link between swing imagery and feel.

mental role in creating the correct swing plane. The body plane—hips, knees and shoulders—created by the set-up is repeatedly overlooked in swing discussion and theory.

In this respect, the plane of the golf swing represents a combination lock. If the combinations of all of the planes—club, upper body and lower body—are aligned and matching, it will simply open up the facility for you to be able to hit the ball far and true. If any of the key planes are misaligned, you will inevitably have to make compensations in your swing as you attempt to unlock the combination and seek a more complicated path to the ball.

Before you delve into this chapter, it is important to remember that images presented over the following pages do not depict the perfect swing plane for you—only the model in the shots. However, they do represent the correct imagery that is needed to create, develop and maintain the plane of the swing. What I have tried to do is create images that are tangible and potent enough to remain locked in your mind as you work on your swing. The best players are aware of the vital link between swing imagery and feel. Less accomplished players also have a relationship between the mind and body, but unfortunately the communication paths are cluttered with useless instructional jargon. This chapter will help clear the way.

Q: WHAT IS SWING PLANE?

A: THE MOST EFFICIENT AND DIRECT ROUTE FROM ADDRESS TO IMPACT

The most efficient swing plane allows the club to move through the most direct route during the swing while constantly relating to the target line. As you address the ball and form your stance and posture as outlined in Law 2, you "punch in" the coordinates that determine your own unique swing plane. Once this is done, the role of the golf swing is to preserve those coordinates during the entire motion—an essential task!

Think of the golf swing as nothing more than a circle on its side.

The relationship between the plane of the swing and the club can be likened to a train and a railway track. The track (the swinging plane) is constant; its path created at address. All the train (the club) has to do is stay on this track to arrive at its final destination (the ball) promptly and efficiently. Sometimes though, the train can run off the rails and, in extreme cases, it can even crash! The further the train moves away from the track, the more difficult it will become to get it back on the rails. With any luck, they may rendezvous at the destination, but more often than not they will pass each other by.

The images in this law will give you an idea of this track, not only with the club, but also the body and the arms. Let these pictures formulate in your mind and remember that, at the end of the day, the golf swing is nothing more than a circle on its side.

YOUR SWING WILL ALWAYS TRY TO FIND ITS IDEAL PLANE

As I mentioned in the introduction, the quality of your swing plane is heavily determined by the angles that you create with your body at address. Finding the correct plane is often a balancing act that becomes disrupted by a lack of discipline at the set-up stage.

If you stand too far away from the ball at address, your swing will automatically adjust to find a more orthodox and comfortable swing path and plane. In this case, it will very often cause you to strike the ball out of the toe of the clubface. Conversely, if you stand too close to the ball, as the swing searches for its proper path, the clubface approaches impact in an open position, causing you to strike the ball out of the heel or, in severe cases, produce a bout of the shanks.

A ONE-PLANE SWING PROVIDES THE ULTIMATE IN CONSISTENCY

It stands to reason that if the golf club swings up and down on the same plane and path, you maximize your chances of striking the ball powerfully and accurately. However, even the most effective and efficient golf swings display a subtle and smooth change of direction between backswing and downswing. This is accompanied by a quite natural shift in plane—by this I mean all of the body planes, including the knees, hips, shoulders, arms, hands and wrists. A dynamically sound swing will possess a slight lowering of the body as the change of direction occurs. This shift in the body's plane is completely natural and is found in many physical activities and sports. A forward kick in karate is only achievable when the supporting leg first squats into the ground to create a power base and source. Tennis players compress their legs into the ground before they spring upwards and launch into a full-blooded serve.

At the start of the downswing as you prepare to hit the ball, your body will instinctively lower its center of gravity in a search for power. It is during this stage that the change in plane occurs. This key power move, which is discussed in more detail in Laws 3 and 6, will essentially shallow and flatten all of the planes, giving the downswing a shallower approach into the ball.

INITIAL PLANE—THE MOST IMPORTANT 12 INCHES OF THE SWING

If a golf swing strays away from orthodoxy, the chances are that it started to go wrong as early as the first foot or so into the backswing. The initial plane does not signify a massive departure from the ball-to-target line—the clubhead scribes the tiniest of arcs away from and through the ball. At this stage of the swing it is imperative that the relationship between the hands and the clubface remains identical to that of the address position. The amount of hand action during this section of the swing should not even register with the brain. The small inside arc is a result of the left arm subtly rotating in a clockwise fashion as you look down at the ball. As the left arm makes this move, the clubface also rotates a little to maintain its square relationship with the arc.

The initial move made by the club is vital to the success of the swing. To avoid tripping up early, avoid these two takeaway sins:

SWING PLANE FLAW 1—THE ROLLING TAKEAWAY

During the initial takeaway, this golfer rolls his hands and wrists excessively outwards and allows them to move too far away from the body, setting the clubhead too far behind the hands when they reach hip height in the backswing. This results in the relationship between the clubhead and the ball-to-target line being destroyed in less than a tenth of a second as the hands hog the limelight.

A strong grip is often responsible for this move. As I explained in Law 1, a great grip provides a "Yin and Yang" relationship. In this case, the strong grip eliminates all sense of unity and balance. This fault can only be eradicated by amending the grip. Only once the hands form a harmonious bond on the club can you create a takeaway that encourages unity.

The "rolling takeaway" demands unreasonable compensations to be made. For example, if the club has rolled off its initial plane by 20 degrees, at some later point during the swing that 20 degrees must be restored in order for the clubface to meet the ball powerfully and efficiently. That is a lot of ground to make up when the club is travelling in excess of 75mph as it approaches impact.

SWING PLANE FLAW 2—THE INSIDE DRAG

In direct contrast to the rolling takeaway, this fault leads to the golfer dragging the clubhead way inside the line—usually with the butt of the club first. Very often this causes the clubface to become hooded and shut. If this golfer's grip was subjected to an autopsy, it would more than likely reveal that the club is held weakly in the palm, denying the golfer any authority over the club. As a result, the club waits for the body to drag it into motion and, in turn, sends it traveling way inside the ball-to-target line. The compensation that is usually required to shift the club back onto the correct plane is an "over the top" movement with the club and body at the start of the downswing, leading to a steep plane and weak, off-line shots.

Remember: "Passive at the beginning and passive at the end," is the motto for the clubhead.

THE CLUBHEAD TOUCHES THE TARGET LINE AT ADDRESS; THE BUTT OF THE CLUB TOUCHES IT DURING THE SWING

At address, the clubhead touches the target line as it is placed behind the ball. However, once the swing begins, it is the butt of the club that relates to the target line until the clubhead once again returns to the ball at impact. A split-second after the ball has been struck, the butt of the club once again restores its relationship with the target line.

The swing plane of the club is determined by its lie angle at address. This does not mean, however, that the club will swing as a mirror image of this address angle. Many golfers mistakenly believe that the angle created at address by the clubshaft must be maintained throughout the swing. This would lead to a very restricted and shallow backswing.

In actual fact, the clubshaft should run parallel to its original address plane throughout the swing, only returning to it at impact. As your arms swing upwards it is inevitable that the club will be lifted on a plane that is higher than the original angle assumed at address. As you will see in the following pages, the butt of the club will work along the target line for the full duration of the backswing with the exception of the first few feet of the takeaway. This is the reason why, when top golfers are playing at their best, the club appears to be in an ever so slightly "laid off" position as they reach the top of the backswing. This is the result of having the butt of the golf club relating to the target line for the longest period possible.

THE SWING PLANE "LINE OF FIRE"

You can easily work on your backswing plane by placing a couple of clubs on the ground directly behind the ball on an extension of the ball-to-target line. This image gives you the correct effect you are after with the butt end of the club. There are three vital reference points to the backswing plane:

INITIAL PLANE

The initial plane refers to the movement of the club during the first 12 inches of the backswing (see page 106). This is when the clubhead is at its most passive. During this early stage it is imperative to maintain the relationship between the clubhead and the hands. There should be no rolling, twisting, lifting or dragging of the clubhead. The only movement is a subtle rotation of the left forearm to initiate a slight inside path away from the ball and ensure that the clubface remains square to the arc during this initial move. This part of the swing is all about starting the club on the correct path. Passivity is the key to mastering the initial plane.

MID-PLANE

By the time your hands, arms and clubshaft have reached mid-plane you will have three key reference points to refer to:

THE MID-PLANE OF THE SWING—IN SYNC AND ON TRACK.

- Looking down at the ball, your left arm should be fairly parallel to—or slightly inside—your toe line. If your left arm is outside or beyond the line of your toes, your chances of blending your arm and body action together are slim.

- As you look down the shaft of the club, the butt should penetrate the ball-to-target line. To check the quality of this position, stick a long pencil into the butt of the club and swing half-way back. If it hits the line, you are in good shape and in the correct position to wind back the body to complete the swing.

- The leading edge of the clubface should be parallel to the angle of the shaft, indicating that it is neutral and square to the plane.

COMPLETION PLANE

As you progress from the mid-plane position, the butt of the club continues to track along the extended ball-to-target line and ensures that the true swinging plane is completed. To check the quality of your backswing plane, pause just before you reach the top of your swing and look along the shaft. The butt should still be pointing at the extended ball-to-target line.

The left forearm also rotates gently during the journey from mid-plane to completion of the backswing. Once again, this subtle move has not only kept the leading edge of the club parallel to the plane, but also kept the arms true to their path as well.

THE CLUBFACE IS SQUARE
TO THE ARM PLANE.
▼

THE ARM PLANE IN BALANCE.
▼

I cannot emphasize strongly enough the importance of continually relating the club to the target line. In order for the swing to function at its best, the club must move on the most direct route back and through while continually relating to the target line. This is why the initial plane is so crucial. Countless instructional articles have been written over the years about the importance of the first 12 inches or so of the backswing because of the chain reaction—good or bad—it creates. Your goal during these early stages is to keep everything as passive as possible.

◀ COMPLETION PLANE—THE BUTT OF THE CLUB AND THE TARGET LINE ALWAYS RELATE.

BODY PLANE

If you have read each chapter in order, you should now appreciate the important function that the body—especially the trunk and the torso—performs during the swing. Although previous coaching theories on swing plane have focused heavily on the role of the hands, arms and the clubshaft, there is no avoiding the issue of body motion. If your body coils around the axis of the spine, great golf is never far away. If, however, your upper body shifts upwards or downwards and disrupts the spine angle created at address, it is nearly impossible to keep the club on plane without some other compensatory movement.

BACKSWING BODY PLANE

The role of the body in the backswing is twofold. Firstly, you wind your body against your legs and the ground to create torque, resistance and power. Secondly, efficient positioning of the body during the backswing will maintain some of those important coordinates that you punched into your posture as you took your address position.

Law 3 addressed the issue of how to create a sturdy yet athletic base for the upper body. Your legs and hips provide the platform upon which your shoulders rotate at a 90-degree angle to your spine. This move is best rehearsed in front of a mirror because the feelings can be very deceptive during the initial learning stage.

DOWNSWING BODY PLANE

As I mentioned earlier, a slight downward motion during the transition between backswing and downswing is the body's natural mechanism for providing a more solid base upon which it can create speed and power.

As this subtle downward shift occurs, you will experience a very slight change in the plane of the body. The clubshaft plane also flattens out, yet remains parallel to the initial backswing plane. In fact, all of the individual body planes will change slightly during this period. However, they all remain parallel to their relative backswing plane. If you ever have the opportunity to watch top golfers in action, you will notice that the divot taken is a slender piece of turf, not the huge clump of earth that many amateur golfers remove from the ground. This is ultimately more achievable if your body planes remain consistent throughout the swing.

THE PLANES OF THE BODY AND THE CLUB.

THE 7 LAWS OF THE GOLF SWING

The golf swing is a chain reaction and much of what occurs at key stages in the backswing is a result of preceding movements and actions. The downswing plane is no exception to this rule. If you can achieve a sound set-up position that encourages a disciplined body motion, you are well on your way to making the downswing move an instinctive reaction.

QUICK TIP: HIT SHOTS WITH BALL ABOVE FEET IN ORDER TO FLATTEN PLANE

If you experience difficulty in "shallowing out" your downswing plane, try hitting some mid-irons from a side-hill lie with the ball above your feet. This immediately gives the body a head start in developing and maintaining a shallow downswing.

◄ FROM LEFT TO RIGHT: THE BACK-SWING BODY PLANE; THE PLANES LOWER AND FLATTEN; MAINTAINING THE PLANES.

ARM PLANES

Many coaches in recent years have placed a huge emphasis on the relationship between the arms and the body during the swing. However, there is a balance to be met. Many club golfers either give their arms too much freedom or they exaggerate the linkage between the arms and the upper body and swing as though their arms are stapled to their chest and their hands glued into their pockets. A great golf swing will always be a blend of hand, arm and body motion. As you can see from the following images, I have broken the arm plane into two sections.

BACKSWING ARM PLANE

The left arm scribes a very small arc to the inside as it moves away from the ball. Looking down at the clubhead resting in the 12 o'clock position at address, you are simply going to move your arms, club and hands to 2 o'clock. You achieve this with a gentle clockwise rotation of the left forearm. Very little else happens during this initial stage of the takeaway. In fact, all you have done is move the exact formation of your hands, arms and clubhead at address to a position just inside of the right foot.

By the time your arms reach hip height, you have a strong indication of how well your backswing is progressing. Looking down at the ball, your left arm should be positioned directly above an imaginary line running across your toes. It is not too disastrous if your left arm is slightly inside this reference point; but only *slightly* inside! However, if your left arm is beyond this boundary, you are in danger of giving your arm swing too much independence from your body. This is also the time to check the club's mid-plane. The shaft of the club should point directly at the ball-to-target line.

On completion of the backswing, your left arm should almost cover the entire shoulder region. This linear relationship places the body in its most resourceful state. Firstly, great arm plane has been achieved, in that a line extended down the left arm would point straight at the ball.

Remember that great plane occurs when each element of the swing aligns to one common focus—the ball-to-target line.

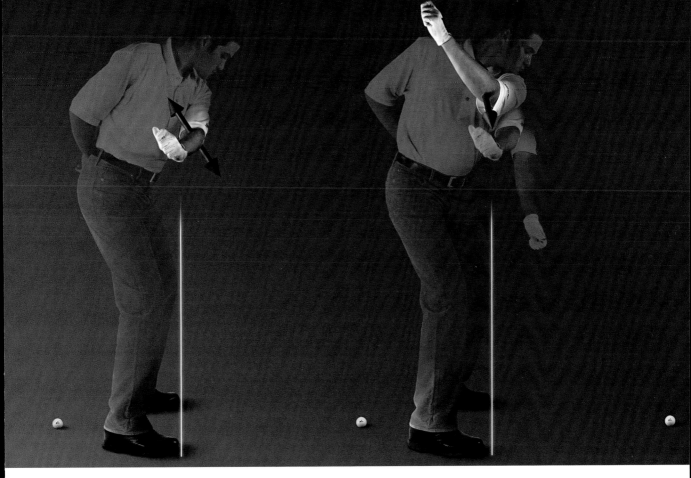

THE SLIGHT INSIDE ARC AND FORE-
ARM ROTATION OF THE LEFT ARM. ▲

Secondly, as the left arm shadows the shoulders it can return back to the ball and take full advantage of the power created by the rotation of the upper body. If your left arm strays above or below the shoulder plane, the line between arms, shoulders and the ball is broken and the arms are forced to work independently from the body during the downswing.

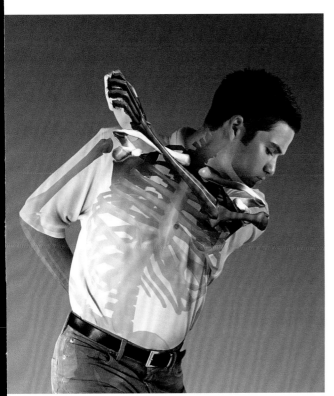

◀ THE LEFT ARM TO SHOULDER PLANE.

DOWNSWING ARM PLANE

Impact is a representation of all the preceding moves during the backswing and downswing. You can see here that the right arm is fairly straight, indicating that it has fully released into the ball. From midway into the downswing to impact the swing is a blur, pretty much uncontrollable and totally at the mercy of the quality of the preceding address position and backswing.

Many golfers view the swing path as a straight line, as it is in snooker or shooting. This is why it is common to see countless amateurs struggling as they try to extend the clubhead down the target line during both the backswing and downswing. This leads to manipulation of the clubhead and an overextended position in the follow-through, neither of which are conducive to great ball-striking.

As you can see here, the plane of the arms scribes an inside path once the ball has been struck, and mirrors the shape and path of the backswing. The right arm travels up through the chest in a circular arc with no attempt whatsoever to follow the ball-to-target line.

It is important to remember that the only straight line in golf is that from the target to the ball and beyond. The clubhead meets that line at address and at impact for a fraction of a second and then moves back inside it in a circular fashion. Never force the clubhead to swing along the ball-to-target line in order to gain more accuracy and control.

Finally, as you reach the end of the swing, your spine angle remains intact and the right arm covers the shoulders. This is simply a carbon copy of the back-swing arm plane. Although your arms will travel slightly further in the down-swing as the momentum of the swing naturally increases the rotation of the upper body, the geometry of everything stays pretty much the same.

◀ IN THIS IMAGE, NOTICE HOW THE SAND HIGHLIGHTS THE ARM PLANE IN THE DOWNSWING THROUGH IMPACT.

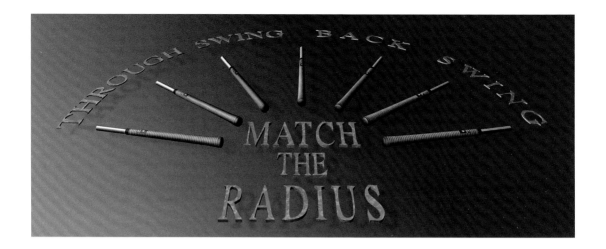

MAINTAIN YOUR RADIUS

This image portrays the arc taken by the grip of the club during the whole swing. As you can see, there is very little variation in the width or arc. Balance is one of the most important keys to a great swing—an overall balance of motion, shape, speed and radius.

Problems occur when this natural swing radius is disrupted or exaggerated. An excessively wide backswing inevitably leads to a narrow downswing as the club attempts to find the "middle ground" at impact. Similarly, a narrow backswing radius will lead to a wider downswing arc as the club instinctively attempts to restore the correct radius.

Paint an image in your mind of the golf swing linked to symmetrical motion. A great golf swing contains several curves, known as "ellipses," which are perfectly symmetrical. Your hands, arms and club travel up and down these tilted 3-D circles during the backswing and down into impact. Clear any thoughts or preconceptions of straight lines being present during the swing from your mind right now.

MAINTAINING SWING RADIUS

It would be folly to think that the body action alone creates the golf swing. While the torso is clearly a key ingredient, some degree of independent arm motion is essential when building a great swing. One of the key roles that the arms play is to maintain a healthy radius. I say "healthy" because every single element of the golf swing can be prone to exaggeration. Ideally, the radius of the swing should be neither too wide nor too narrow to function at its best. The effect we need to achieve with the arms is clearly shown in the images overleaf.

RIGHT ARM FOLD

In the early stages of the backswing and the follow-through, the arms knit close against the body. However, this does not mean that they are jammed into the side of the upper body. Instead, they are pliable and fold like hinges during these key stages of the swing. These images show why it is possible, indeed recommended, to play chip and pitch shots with the arms totally linked to the body pivot. The smaller swing can sustain a total "blend" of arm swing and body turn.

RIGHT ARM WING

As the swing progresses, however, you must give your arms their independence. From the mid-point of the backswing, allow your right arm to spread slightly and move away from the body. As this occurs, the slight stretching feeling signifies that the top of the backswing has been achieved. If you have created good resistance on your right leg, you should also sense that the entire left side of your upper body is being pulled in response to the torque and coil created. This move ensures that three key things happen:

- **The hands remain in between the shoulders, as they were at address, throughout the backswing.**

- **The radius of the swing is maintained.**

- **The left arm is prevented from swinging too far inside the target line.**

LEFT ARM FOLD/LEFT ARM WING

Through impact and slightly beyond, your arms should maintain a close working relationship with your body. As the swing progresses past mid-plane, and the arms start to swing up the chest in the final moments of the through swing, your left arm will start to separate from the body—just as your right arm did on the backswing.

If you have been guilty in the past of attempting to eradicate all involvement of the arms during the swing, this new information will give you a sense of freedom and room throughout the whole swing and especially at impact. The "hit" will suddenly feel easier to accomplish and an increased speed in the arms and the hands will also become apparent.

SUMMARY—CLOSE THE GAP BETWEEN WHAT YOU ARE FEELING AND WHAT YOU ARE ACTUALLY DOING

Because the torso is a large, physical mass, making changes to its motion can be relatively quick and painless. The arms and the golf club, however, present a different predicament. Positioning the club correctly during the swing requires good synchronization with the body motion as well as the ability to develop great awareness of where the club is at any given point without directly looking at it.

When working on the shape of your swing, bear the following two factors in mind. Assuming that your swing is well synchronized, your ultimate goal is to close the gap between what you are feeling and what you are actually doing. Your coach can help greatly in this department by using an awareness exercise where you both judge the quality of the swing move attempted and give a score out of ten. Always remember that since your coach can monitor your swing motion far more effectively than you can, his grade is likely to be the more accurate.

RIGHT ARM FOLD.   RIGHT ARM WING.

When a 10/10 mark is given by both parties, you will know that you have not only achieved the correct position, but that the feeling you experienced accurately reflected what happened in the swing. Where possible, always ask your coach to use a video camera in this type of situation, both as a back-up for his judgement and for your peace of mind.

The golf swing moves in a series of arcs, each one a different size. I hope that Law 5 has given you some simple yet powerful images to reinforce this and help you to build and maintain your golf swing, in particular to the ideal journey undertaken by the golf club. This should be the most economical route away from and back to the ball at impact—a true one-plane golf swing.

Finally, make sure that you avoid falling into the trap of thinking that the term "one-plane" means that the angle of the clubshaft should remain the same as at address throughout the swing. This is merely a starting point. From address onwards, the club and left arm track up the height of the body, but will always relate to that original line. Once you have completed your well-coordinated and powerful backswing it is time to move onto Law 6—Firing into the Ball.

LEFT ARM FOLD.   LEFT ARM WING.

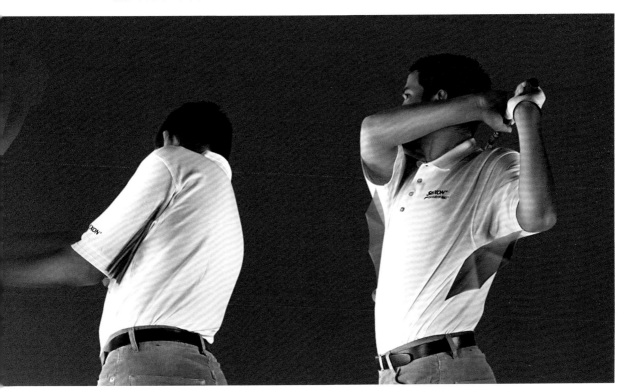

LAW 6

FIRING INTO THE BALL
Releasing all you have

INTRODUCTION

When you are taught to shoot a rifle or a bow and arrow, the instructor will almost certainly place a great deal of emphasis on the moment before the bullet or arrow is released. In the case of the rifle, the instructor will stress the importance of squeezing the trigger gently in order to achieve maximum accuracy and efficiency. Once the arrow has been drawn back, it is essential to steady the diaphragm by momentarily holding your breath before letting go. Both of these examples indicate a moment of poise before allowing the power that has been created to be delivered towards the intended target. The composure is an integral component of a well-rehearsed and disciplined send-off. The calm before the storm!

This law will show you how to apply a similar philosophy to starting your downswing. It will provide your body with the necessary timing to coordinate all of the assets that you have created thus far during the backswing. It almost goes without saying, however, that the role of the downswing is made considerably easier when the previous laws have been adhered to. In the perfect golf swing, the downswing should be reaction without thought.

Composure is an integral component of a well-rehearsed and disciplined send-off.

THE TRUTH ABOUT THE DOWNSWING

The downswing has traditionally been viewed as dangerous, fragile and volatile. For almost a century now, the question of what actually starts the downswing has consumed thousands of players and coaches around the world. This question refers to the correct sequencing of the downswing and will finally be answered overleaf by the "step in" drill. This exercise represents the simplest and most effective way to learn the correct order of movement and the flowing nature of a great downswing.

If there is a mantra for a great downswing it is this: **"Restore every move you have made during the backswing plus a little bit more to reach impact."** As you will discover, your address position is not a mirror image of your impact position! This all too common and erroneous belief has had a dramatic effect upon golf swings around the world. Unlike the square, 50/50 balance found in a regular address position, a good impact position sees the left side of the body slightly open to the target line with the weight slightly forward, allowing the right side to fire through. This is the "little bit more" that the mantra refers to. Whatever you put into the backswing you must make sure that you replace it on the way down.

PRACTICE EXERCISE: THE "STEP IN" DRILL

The transference of weight from the right side of the body to the left should be one continuous movement. The best golf swings flow; they do not stop and start. This exercise is designed to help you feel the fluid transition from backswing to downswing.

- Take a mid-iron and address the ball, which you should play an inch ahead of your left foot, with a very narrow stance.

- Make a smooth backswing and when you sense that you are ready to start your downswing, allow your left foot to step to the left side of the ball. In reality, your left leg should start to move before you reach the top of your backswing.

- As your weight naturally settles into your left side, fire your body through the ball into your finish position.

- Repeat this drill a number of times and really try to pick up on the "wave" like motion that will start to come to you after a few shots. This is probably one of the greatest rhythm drills a golfer can perform to really create flowing downswing.

PLANTING THE LEFT LEG PILLAR IN THE DOWNSWING

During Law 3, I highlighted the similarities between the leg action of a boxer and that of a golfer during the transition between backswing and downswing. Both demonstrate a very fluid passing of power and weight transference from the right leg to the left.

You may be surprised to learn that this move, which is present in every good golf swing, is already well within your grasp. As you walk from one side of the room to the other, you are making exactly the same transitional move from the right side of the body to the left that is required during the change of direction in the golf swing. The only difference is that, during the golf swing itself, this movement is a little more dynamic.

The left side of the body acts as a pillar that has to be planted before the right side of the body can slam into it.

As I discussed earlier, the very same leg action can be seen in many other sports, including karate, baseball and tennis. In effect, the left leg simply prepares the hitting area for the right side of the body to "fire" into. At the start of the downswing, the left side of the body acts as a pillar that has to be planted before the right side of the body can slam into it. Without this firm left side there is no discipline or control over the downswing motion and no resistance for the right side of the body to hit against.

Typical slicers allow the right side of their body to become involved far too early in the downswing, leading to that all too familiar out-to-in swing path through the ball. Similarly, golfers who drive their hips excessively at the start of the downswing and inevitably push or hook the ball will benefit from planting the left leg rather than allowing it to slide forwards. Once this has been achieved the player can then rotate into the left leg rather than slide into it.

LEVEL BELT LINE GIVES ARMS FREEDOM IN THE DOWNSWING

As the golf swing pulls into reverse, it gathers all of the assets that it has amassed in preparation for impact and beyond. The role of the body at this vital stage of the swing is to fully release all of its torque and power while providing stability, balance and a commitment to fully completing the swing.

A disciplined body motion will permit total freedom in the arm-swing during the downswing. In this context, discipline and freedom go hand in hand and this is a combination well worth working on. Indeed, your hands and arms will only find the freedom to hit the ball powerfully if the body rotates correctly. Keeping your belt line level is a key to creating the correct motion. If your belt line becomes tilted and rocks the spine backward, the right arm jams into the right side of your body, where it becomes trapped and weak.

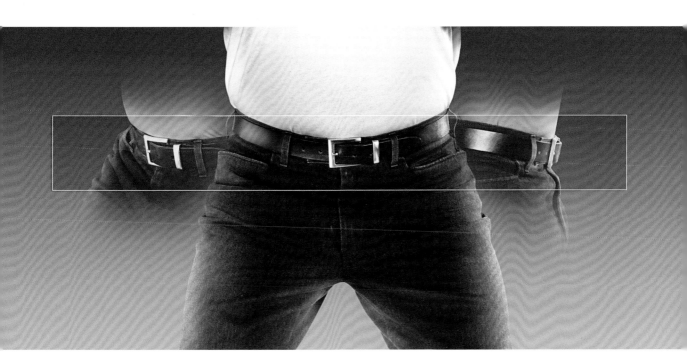

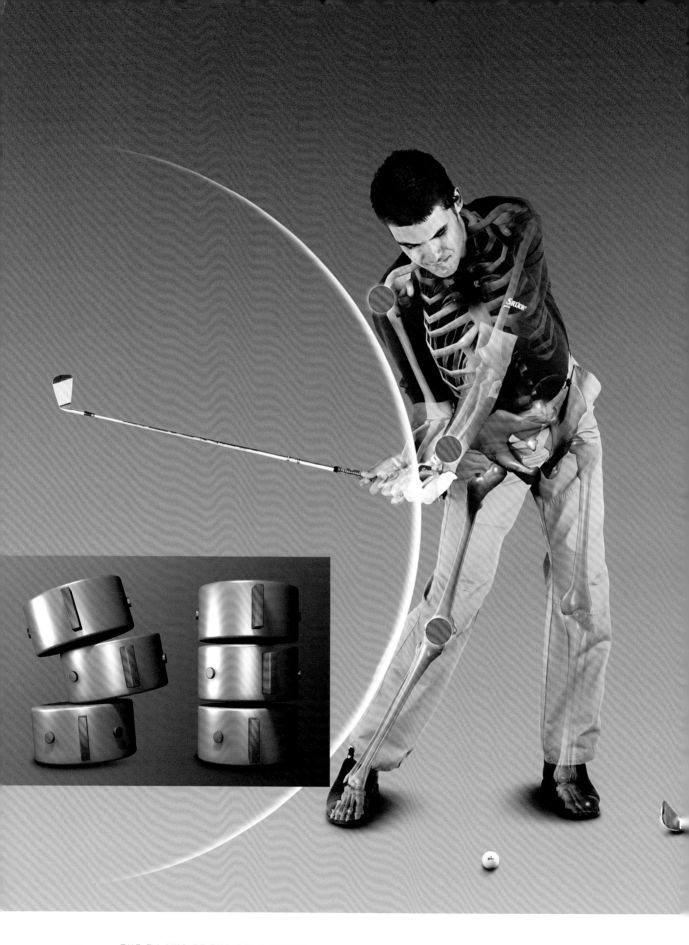

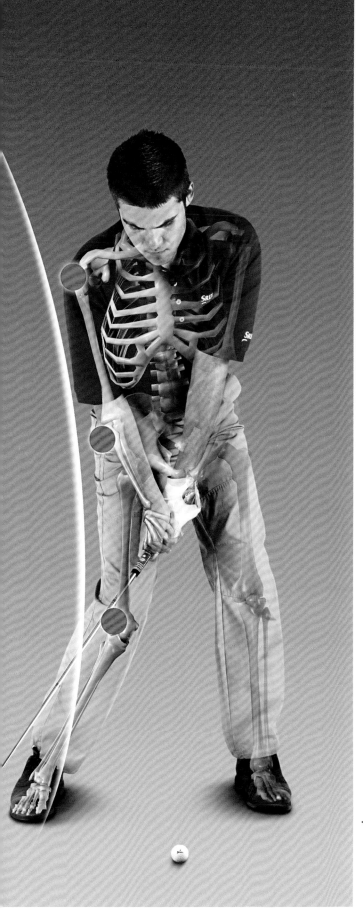

THE TRUTH BEHIND THE DREADED "REVERSE C" FINISH

One of my main objectives in writing this book was to uncover and explain some of the most commonly used phrases in golf terminology. However, simply offering a description of a swing trait or fault is not enough—it needs to be analyzed and then revealed for what it is and how it affects the golf swing.

The term "Reverse C" finish is a casual description of the backward arching of the spine through impact and into the follow-through that, as the term suggests, resembles the shape of a reversed letter "C." It is amazing to think that this position, which is created by excessive leg and hip action in the downswing, was taught as a desirable finish in the late 1960s and 1970s. It is little wonder that so many golfers from that era now suffer from spine-related injuries.

◀ LEFT: THE "REVERSE C" FINISH. RIGHT: THE KEY JOINTS FALL INTO LINE. FAR LEFT: A BARREL REPRESENTATION OF BOTH FINISHING POSITIONS.

THE "REVERSE C"—KEY JOINTS MOVE OUT OF LINE

An excessive hip and leg drive at the start of the downswing causes the relationship between the shoulders, arms and knees to break down. If you look closely at the image on the previous page, you will see that the major joints of the right side of the body have fallen out of line and that the body is in an unbalanced and unstable position.

The downward lurch with the hips and knees effectively forces the sternum backwards, thereby setting the low point of the swing too far behind the ball and bringing all kinds of poorly struck shots into play. The end result is that the hands and arms are forced to play catch up and, invariably, the player will have to rely on a "flicky" release with the wrists in order to square the blade at impact—a method that is not particularly conducive to producing consistent golf.

THE CORRECT LEVEL FINISH—KEY JOINTS FALL INTO LINE

The right leg has to wait before it can become involved in the downswing. If it is activated too early, the legs are literally whipped away from underneath the torso. In the second image, you can see how every major joint in the right side of the body falls into line with the rest. This produces a shallow attack into the ball and well-struck shots time after time. Another welcome benefit is of course the reduction of the possibility of injury.

If you suspect that your finish resembles that of a "Reverse C" you should repeat the "step in" drill on page 127. This exercise is designed specifically to teach the right leg to fire in only when the left has prepared the hitting area. Also, pay specific attention to the quality of your belt line through the ball. An overzealous thrust of the right leg has probably tilted this vital area of the swing.

APPLIED LEVERAGE—OPEN AND CLOSE YOUR LEVER FOR POWER AND ACCURACY

Your arms act as levers in the golf swing in that they close and contract to generate power and then open and extend to deliver it. I refer to this as "applied leverage" and it is this action that you need to encourage in the right arm.

Whereas the left arm can be used as a guide to indicate the quality of the swing plane during the backswing, the right arm assumes this role in the downswing. The action of the right arm in the

OPENING UP THE JOINTS OF THE RIGHT ARM INTO IMPACT.

golf swing is analogous with that used to throw a ball. The right arm gathers power going back (the lever closes) and propels the ball away (the lever opens). Entering the impact area with the arm still fully loaded with these angles will lead to a volatile and inconsistent action with the hands through the ball. The release of the right arm must occur in one smooth motion from the top to the bottom of the swing ensuring that the power delivered is done so with optimum control over the clubface.

As you can see from this image, the actual point of "hit" during the downswing is depicted soon after impact. This occurs for two very good reasons. The first is that the position of the "Hit Hard" sign represents the area in which the clubhead should be traveling at maximum speed. Remember that the downswing is a gradual increase of momentum that climaxes shortly after the ball has been struck. This way, you can guarantee that the clubhead is accelerating through impact. Secondly, it is important to understand that you do not hit at the ball, but through it. A great golf swing simply captures the ball in its path.

PRACTICE EXERCISE: LOSE YOUR RIGHT ANGLES!

The best way to tackle any improvement or fault in the golf swing is to isolate the area in question. In this case, swinging with just the right hand allows you to train the correct right arm release, while also encouraging the right side of the body to release and fire through.

- Take a 7-iron and tee the ball up. Place your left hand on your right shoulder and hover the clubhead just in front of the ball. Swing smoothly to the top of your backswing, allowing your right arm to close and hinge back.

- In the downswing, your focus is to release the two angles that you have created in the elbow and wrist joints. You should feel your right arm gradually "open up" as it accelerates into the ball and beyond.

UNDERSTANDING IMPACT

The ideal impact position is often seen as something elusive and magical. While it is not something that you should consciously attempt to replicate or force during your swing, it is important nonetheless to familiarize yourself with the qualities of a great impact position.

During the process of learning and playing golf there is no greater resource to call upon than your imagination. Words are never enough when describing and teaching the game. In fact, things are positively at their worst when the power of imagery is substituted for meaningless and often confusing verbosity.

A clear image of a coordinated downswing is worth more than a thousand words when it comes to understanding what constitutes a great impact position. I believe that it is best to view impact as a part of a larger whole, especially if you have been guilty of overemphasizing its importance or identifying it as the only key position in the golf swing.

It is often said that the one thing a golfer has to do correctly to become a proficient striker of the ball is to achieve a good impact position. Although this may appear to be the case in some very idiosyncratic swings, the "one thing" is almost certainly not impact, but instead an earlier move or position that in turn produces the qualities necessary for great impact.

The key is not to view impact as the main focus of the swing, but rather as a position that you must pass through en route to completion. The ball must not be hit at, but rather collected.

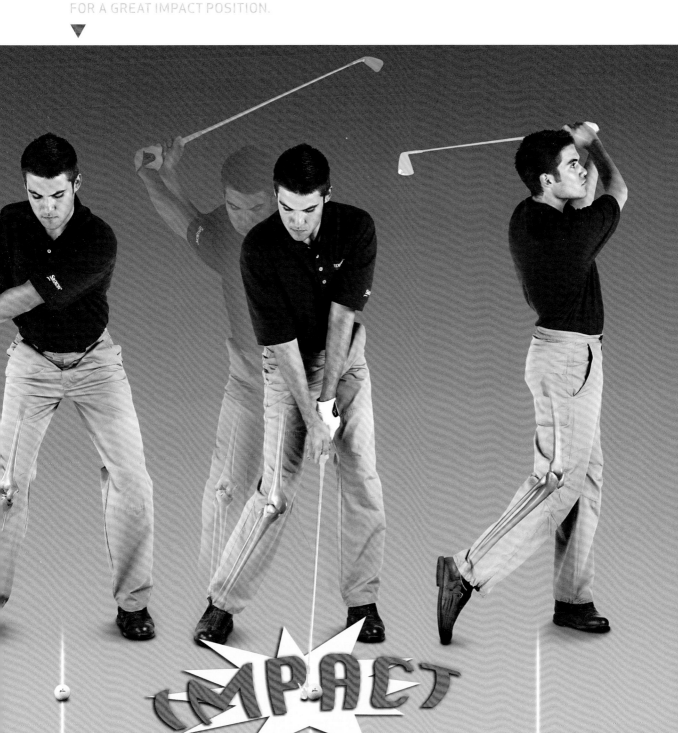

THE THREE KEYS TO PERFECT IMPACT

Ultimately, coordination in the golf swing is determined by the quality of the relationship between the clubhead and the body. Nowhere is this coordination more important than at impact when the clubface strikes the ball.

- Your sternum represents the ballistics of the strike.
- Your body has partially opened up to the target.
- Your right knee and the clubhead have reached the impact line together.

The image on page 136 encompasses all of these great impact qualities in one simple drill. It will also encourage the whole of the right side of your body to work through the ball and beyond. Problems occur when the right side—and in particular the right knee—hangs back, allowing everything else to flip by and release uncontrollably past impact.

Start by making some half swings, ideally using a video camera or a mirror, to feel the link between the clubhead and the right knee coming into the impact line. Gradually increase the length and speed of the swing until you are confident that you can achieve the correct movement within your normal full swing. After a short while you will begin to feel that you can hit the ball as hard as you like as long as the right side of the body actively fires forwards.

THE SECRET TO HITTING THE BALL HARD—COORDINATE RIGHT KNEE AND CLUBHEAD

It must be a complete mystery to many golfers how the world's top players are able to strike the ball with an equal amount of aggression and control. Of these two factors, control should be your primary goal; however, there are times when an injection of power can significantly alter your scoring potential.

When you do want to press for those extra yards the worst thing you can do is allow your swing to become tight and rigid. Instead, wind up a smooth backswing that feels even longer and more languid than normal and ensure that the start of the downswing begins in exactly the same fashion. This takes care of the power part of the equation.

The control of this power comes from fully committing the right side of the body into the shot. When you want the clubhead to move through impact with speed, your right knee and foot must accompany it. Always remember that since the clubhead will be moving far faster than the body at this stage of the swing, you must fire your body through equally as hard. You can develop this essential coordination by starting with some gentle pitch shots and then gradually applying the same philosophy throughout the bag.

LEARN TO RELEASE EVERYTHING

In Law 4, I explained how you should be looking to use your hands consistently during the entire motion of the golf swing rather than at one or two specific points. This ensures that the blend of hand, arm and body motion has the very best chance of working in unison.

When the term "release" is used in relation to the golf swing, it is very important to understand that it refers to everything being released into the ball and not just the hands. I also must stress at this juncture that the hands should never be "rolled" through impact in an effort to square the clubface to the target. This all too common belief originates from hordes of slicers trying in vain to become drawers of the ball. The fact is that a great grip (square clubface) coupled with sound body motion (consistency in motion) and good synchronization (good positioning of the club and timing) will almost completely eliminate any chance of slicing the ball. These qualities are readily available to you and can all be found in the previous 5 laws.

THE "PUCK" RELEASE—YOUR KEY TO STRAIGHTER, LONGER SHOTS

If you cast your mind back to Law 1, you will remember that your grip has two primary functions. The first is to align and blend the hands onto the clubface. The second is to deliver the clubhead powerfully into the ball at impact. For both of these objectives to be achieved in one swift movement, a certain type of release must take place through the hitting area. I refer to this as the "puck release" because of the resemblance it bears to the way in which an ice hockey player propels the puck forward. It would be beneficial here to take a closer look at how this release ensures that the clubhead remains true to the target line and the plane of the swing.

The best swings incorporate very little in the way of hand and forearm rotation through the ball.

Erratic golfers roll their hands and forearms over each other through the impact area. Releasing the club in this fashion leads to inconsistent ball-striking and a lack of control over the direction of the shot. I am not saying that there should be no hand and forearm rotation during the swing—there most certainly is—but it takes place during the last moments of the backswing and the last moments of the follow-through when the extra rotation is required to keep the club on plane. The best swings however, incorporate very little in the way of hand and forearm rotation through the ball.

In all good swings, the right wrist joint and the right arm straighten as they deliver the club to impact. The momentum of this action will naturally continue unless it is physically interrupted. The right hand will work slightly under the left hand after striking the ball and, in doing so, will keep the clubface square to the target and on the optimum plane for the longest possible time.

PRACTICE EXERCISE: TRAIN THE PUCK RELEASE WITH LITTLE CHIPS

To cultivate the correct sensation of the puck release, first rehearse the motion by hitting a series of chip shots building up to longer swings.

- Take an 8-iron and set up to play a short-range chip with your weight just favoring your front foot.

THE "PUCK" RELEASE, WHICH CAN HELP YOU ▶
TO MAKE STRAIGHTER AND LONGER SHOTS.

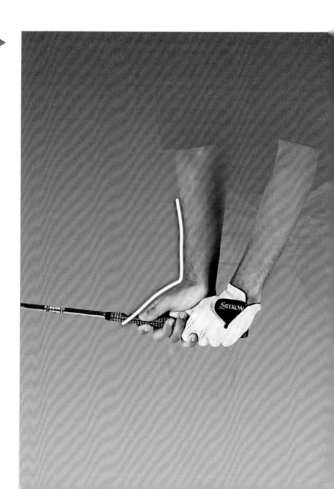

- As you initiate your backswing, allow your right wrist to hinge back on itself.

- Starting back down, gently release this angle so that your right hand works underneath the left through impact.

- After about 10 repetitions, progress to making half-swings with your 8-iron and eventually a full swing, making sure that you continue to release your right hand in exactly the same way each time. You will be pleasantly surprised at the level of control you now possess over the release and flight of the ball.

QUASHING THE MYTH OF THE SCOOP

This method of releasing the hands through the ball may be a confusing concept for many readers who are probably thinking that what I have just advocated is a scooping action through impact and the perfect way to dig the clubhead into the ground behind the ball. This would certainly be the case if the body is incorrectly positioned at impact. For example, if the hips slide forward and send the spine falling backwards away from the target then it is very easy to hit too far behind the ball and catch the shot heavy.

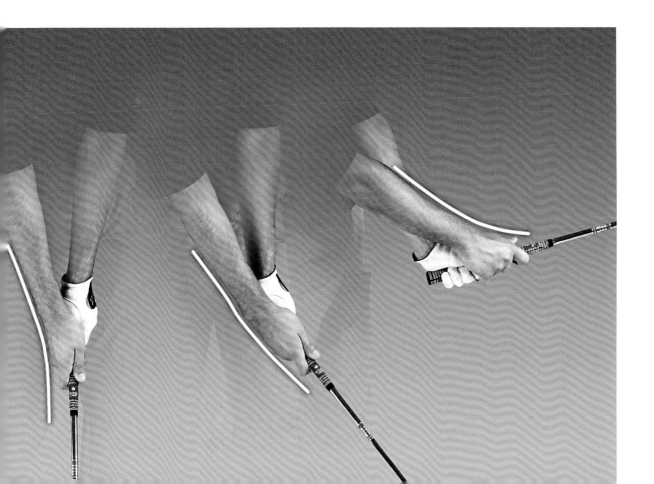

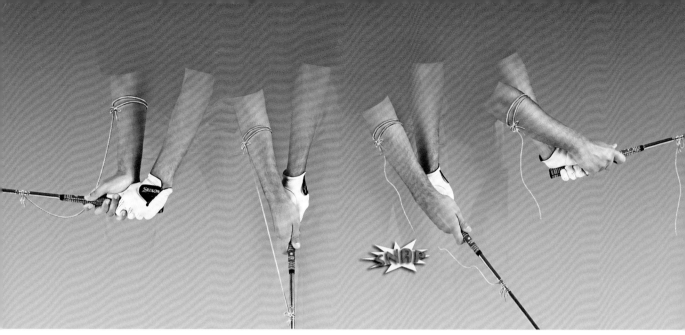

KEEP THIS IMAGE IN MIND WHEN YOU PRACTICE.
SNAP THE STRING FOR A POWERFUL STRIKE.

However, it is almost impossible to "duff" the ball if your body has prepared and positioned itself into the impact area with conviction. The puck release is one of the most closely guarded secrets among the world's top players. You will immediately see its straightening effect on the ball even as you carry out the small, 8-iron chip shots.

NOW YOU CAN HIT HARD WITH COMPLETE CONFIDENCE

During the course of the past century, many top golfers have commented that they can use the right hand aggressively through impact. They can, it seems, freely release the right forearm without suffering any loss of control. Once your confidence and skill levels increase, you will be able to use the puck release to hit the ball astonishingly hard with the right hand, while keeping the clubface square to the target.

FEEDBACK FROM YOUR FINISH

Always try to hold your finish momentarily after the ball has been struck whatever the outcome of the shot. Apart from ensuring that discipline and balance have been present throughout the whole motion it also gives the body a chance to receive some vital feedback from the swing itself. Stillness is the key to receiving feedback from the body. This is vital to the learning process, though more subconsciously than consciously. With stillness, the body will reliably send information about the swing back to your brain.

UNDERSTANDING RHYTHM AND TEMPO

RHYTHM IS MECHANICAL; TEMPO IS PERSONAL
RHYTHM IS THE "ONE-TWO" OF A SWING; TEMPO IS THE
SPEED OF THE "ONE-TWO"

The above statements are just about the simplest way to describe the speed of any golf swing. Understanding the exact differences between rhythm and tempo and recognizing what effects they have upon the golf swing will release the freedom for many golfers to hit the ball well. Countless players continually struggle to find a consistent swing speed that suits their game. Frankly, it's easy to see why it is so frustrating for the golfer who is not entirely in the picture. So what comes first—rhythm or tempo? The answer is firstly to gain better rhythm through better technique. Good technique represents equality in the overall motion, shape and size of your swing. Rhythm is born out of this consistency of motion.

You should never try to manipulate or force tempo. As discussed in Law 4, tempo is built into your system, psyche and physical make-up. If you continually focus on achieving a "one-two" rhythm when you practice, the correct swing tempo swing will follow. This is why good technique followed by rhythm must be your priority.

FINDING YOUR IDEAL TEMPO—BRING YOUR SWING SPEED RATIOS TOGETHER

The easiest way to discover your "natural" tempo is to understand the relationship between the speed of the backswing and the downswing. For example, if you attempt to swing the club back slowly, you will inevitably snatch the club back down into the ball as you instinctively try to find a faster gear. This type of swing can be represented by the following ratio: Backswing 20 mph: Downswing 70 mph. Here, the difference in speed between backswing and downswing is far too great.

You will find your ideal tempo by moving these swing speeds closer together. Something like: Backswing 55 mph: Downswing 70 mph. This will allow your swing to align itself to your natural personality far more effectively. These figures are not totally accurate for every golfer, but they do provide a good starting point. Simply forming the image in your mind of the two elements of the swing blending together like this will allow your golf swing to develop its own rhythm for the very first time.

RHYTHM PROBLEMS

Q: Golfer A has never received any kind of golf tuition and his swing is a myriad of different directions and speeds. His swing thoughts vary from week to week. Why is it that this golfer has poor inconsistent rhythm from one swing to the next?

A: Quite simply because he has no rhythm! Rhythm can only be created when the technical elements of the swing combine to create a free-flowing motion. Many professional golfers have swings that contain some quirky movements, but certain technical factors unite to make them work. However, you will find that these golfers have to practice twice as hard as the players with exemplary technique to ensure that the strength of their rhythm compensates for the quirkiness of their technique.

TEMPO PROBLEMS

Q: Suspecting that he is a victim of swinging the club too quickly, Golfer B pays several visits to his driving range. During every single practice session he focuses on pacifying the pace of his swing until he feels that he has cultivated a slower motion. Eager to try out his newly grooved slower swing, he steps onto the golf course at the weekend and swipes at the ball violently. His head is soon in his hands as he loses all sense of feel and control in his swing. Why could he not sustain his slower tempo?

A: Golfer B believes that he is doing the right thing by fighting his quick tempo, but he really needs to take a look at himself. If he talks quickly, thinks quickly and drives quickly it is no surprise that he should swing quickly, too. Conversely, a golfer who is methodical and deliberate in nature off the course is likely to have a swing that matches his personality traits.

SUMMARY

The freedom to hit the ball hard, safe in the knowledge that you have directional control, is a liberating feeling. The primary mission of Law 6 is to make the journey from the top of the backswing back down to impact and beyond as uninhibited as possible. Any golfer with the ability to strike the ball long and straight will undoubtedly possess all of the qualities found within this chapter.

As the golf swing pulls into reverse, it should replace every move that has taken place during the backswing with particular emphasis placed upon swing synchronization due to the amount of force and speed generated in the swing. Law 4 demonstrated that the body must give the club a head start during the backswing to compensate for the extra distance that it has to travel. The "step in" drill (see page 127) gives the body this same waiting period at the start of the downswing, where it momentarily stalls and waits for the clubhead to catch up prior to striking the ball.

This is an exercise that will benefit the typical slicer, as it will give the right arm the time and opportunity to release and straighten onto the correct plane and path. The problems for the hooker usually stem from the body, too. Images such as the "Reverse C" and the "hip tilt" found in Law 3 show vividly how, when the body fails to rotate correctly, the right arm can become trapped against it.

Ironically, the end of this summary starts with a backswing thought. When the opportunity arises to cut loose with a big drive, you must allow the swing to gather itself fully before starting its journey down. In a career that included 18 professional Major championships, one swing thought served Jack Nicklaus better than any other: complete the backswing. It is imperative that you do not rush the backswing or downswing when you are under pressure or seeking a few extra yards. Remember, timing is everything.

This chapter summarizes most of the mechanical information that will enable you to take your game to a higher level. I say "most" because a fundamentally sound swing only gives you the potential to play super golf, not the right to it—as you will discover in Law 7—Dance with the Target.

LAW 7

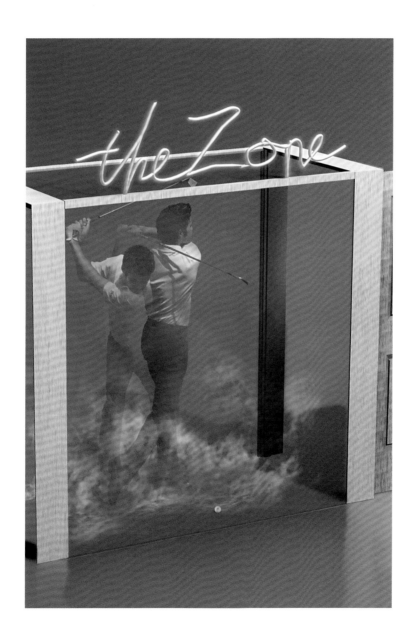

DANCE WITH THE TARGET
Switch off the mind and turn on the body

INTRODUCTION

The laws presented so far in this book have been sequential with regard to the order in which I believe you should build a consistent and technically orthodox golf swing. While each of these laws has assumed equal importance, the seventh and final law represents a totally different kind of lesson. The previous six laws have focused primarily on swing technique, but the information contained in this chapter will help you to combine what you have learned into one free-flowing, spontaneous series of movements.

Now that you have a greater understanding of the physicality of the golf swing, what your game needs now is a pulse—a lifeblood of motion that will enable it to function at its very best. In this chapter you will learn how to create habits and routines that will provide a stimulus for your golf swing and, in time, dictate the way in which you act from the moment you arrive at the ball until you see your shot disappear into the distance.

It is vital that you do not underestimate the importance of consistent pre-shot preparation. If you need further evidence of just how crucial these routines are, you simply need to study the mannerisms of any Tour pro who has achieved significant success over an extended period of time. Players such as Jack Nicklaus, Tiger Woods, Nick Price and Nick Faldo all have distinctive pre-shot routines that will have varied very little, if at all, throughout their entire careers.

Most of these routines include personal little mannerisms, such as a quick tug of the trouser leg or shirt collar, a waggle of the clubhead, a shuffle of the feet or a forward press of the hands before starting the backswing. These are nothing more than signals for the mind to switch from its analytical mode into the subconscious automotive state that allows the body to focus purely on the process of hitting the ball toward the target without the intervention of cumbersome and often destructive thoughts.

It is vital that you do not underestimate the importance of consistent pre-shot preparation.

That is not to say that your pre-shot routine should contain no conscious thought whatsoever. Far from it, in fact. Every solid and consistent pre-shot routine should start with a fully conscious assessment of the shot that you are about to play. I refer to this mental process as "filling up the bottle" and I will explain this concept in more detail a little later.

The key lesson to learn from this chapter is to resist the temptation to interfere with the habit-forming process. If you have designed an intelligent pre-shot routine that incorporates the required analytical and spontaneous elements, then this is all you can expect from yourself. However, some golfers refuse to trust their routine or continually try to refine the smallest detail at the expense of destroying the larger whole. This is rather like a bad gardener who throws a seed into the ground only to dig it up a week later in order to check on its progress. If you choose to continually fiddle with your routine you will continually struggle with your game. Choose a routine and stick with it through thick and thin. I promise you it will be worth it.

FILLING UP THE BOTTLE—THE CONSCIOUS SIDE OF YOUR PRE-SHOT ROUTINE

A routine in golf is nothing more than a well-rehearsed series of motions and actions that take place before the ball is struck. A good pre-shot routine allows your subconscious to assume control over the shot. However, every pre-shot routine must begin with a conscious analysis of the shot you are about to play. Only once you have absorbed and processed all the necessary information required to help you plan your shot can you allow yourself to slip into autopilot and allow your subconscious to take over.

Before the shot is assessed your mind is similar to an empty bottle. If it remains empty, any manner of destructive thought can enter into it, destroying any chance of success. Standing over the ball with your mind full of self-doubt and negative thoughts is hardly the kind of mental state that is conducive to playing good golf. These doubts can arise from questioning your physical ability to play a particular shot, an uncertainty over the choice of shot that you are taking on, a lack of clarity in your thinking or an oversight in your decision-making process.

I believe that the purpose of the analytical part of your pre-shot routine is to "fill up your bottle of confidence." In order to stand over the ball positively and with total faith in your ability and your choice of shot, you must ensure that this bottle is full. If there is any room at all left in the bottle, the gap will be filled with negative and potentially destructive thoughts.

YOUR PRE-FLIGHT CHECKLIST

There are four primary factors that you must examine and analyze before you can develop the feeling of confidence and conviction that is vital to positive and successful shot-making.

Just as a pilot will run through a pre-flight checklist before he attempts to fly a plane, all good golfers have a similar mental process that they will run through prior to playing any shot. In doing so, they are embarking on a decision-making process that, if adhered to on the golf course and on the practice range, will add consistency to their game.

At this stage, do not be too concerned if you make a few mental errors in your decision-making since this is an integral element of the learning process. The whole purpose of this exercise, however, is to avoid the act of kicking yourself for making avoidable errors—you must learn from any such mistakes. The four key points listed below run in a specific order that is designed to make your decision-making as accurate as possible.

You may find it useful to write these four shot factors down on your glove, yardage chart or somewhere on the scorecard. As long as you stick to the process of asking yourself these crucial questions it won't be too long before they become a natural part of your pre-shot routine.

1   Examine the lie of the ball to determine what type of shot is possible.
2   Assess the wind and other factors that will affect the flight of the ball, such as slopes and elevation.
3   Designate your targets—starting target and finishing target.
4   Calculate the correct yardage to the hole or intended target.

Once the "bottle" is full and you have a clear picture in your mind of how you want to play the shot, the conscious part of your pre-shot routine is completed. Now you need to allow your subconscious mind to take over and complete the rest of the routine. To facilitate this transition between conscious and unconscious thought you need a physical trigger.

PHYSICAL TRIGGERS—YOUR LINK BETWEEN CONSCIOUS AND UNCONSCIOUS THOUGHT

With a well-rehearsed pre-shot routine you can make the act of hitting a golf ball as habitual as riding a bike, but you must be prepared to let go of control at the right time. This is where the difficulty lies for many golfers because there is such a short period of time between assessing the shot that you want to play before switching the conscious mind off and allowing the subconscious to take over.

A physical trigger sends out a message of readiness to the brain.

In order to slip seamlessly from your conscious mode of thought into your subconscious pre-shot routine, it is important to create a link or a trigger which, if practiced enough times, will prompt this transition and instantly send the body into a state of automation that will allow you to approach and hit the ball without any obstructive thoughts or mental interferences.

A physical trigger sends out a message of readiness to the brain. By this stage, all of your pre-shot preparation must have been completed. If you have not successfully filled up the bottle, the remaining space left will become occupied by doubts, insecurities and negative thoughts. Here are two physical triggers that you can use to tap into a desirable "mental" state time and time again.

PRIMING THE CLUB—SHAKE AND GO

Once you have carefully taken your grip, take one more look at the target from behind the ball. Use this valuable time to compose yourself and take a good deep breath. This will slow your heart rate down a little and reduce tension, especially in your upper body.

Now is the time to use your physical trigger. While still locked into the target, subtly shake the club towards and away from your body. As you do this, allow your grip pressure to increase a little as you feel the weight of the clubhead in your hands. When the club settles start your walk into the ball. Your routine has begun.

PRIME BOTH THE MIND AND THE CLUB FOR ACTION.

These small, almost imperceptible mannerisms… can form the foundation of a robust pre-shot routine.

TWEAK THE GLOVE— A QUICK TUG SETS THE TONE

An alternative physical trigger that is equally effective is to gently tug on your golf glove. Again, take one final look at the target from behind the ball as you draw in a deep breath. When you have delivered the club into your left hand, you will have time to grab the cuff of the glove with your right hand and give it a small tug while still focusing on your target. This action is your physical trigger. Now start your walk into the ball by fitting your right hand on top of the left to complete your grip.

Although you may feel that these small, almost imperceptible, mannerisms are minor and just another unnecessary thing to think about before you play your shot, I can assure you that if you practice them regularly enough, they can form the foundation of a robust and unshakeable pre-shot routine.

A GENTLE TWEAK OF THE GLOVE CAN ACT AS AN EFFECTIVE PHYSICAL TRIGGER TO START YOUR PRE-SHOT ROUTINE.

Bear in mind, however, that these are just two simple examples. You may wish to integrate one of the above triggers into your pre-shot routine, or you may prefer to create your own personal key. There is certainly room for experimentation, but whichever trigger you decide to use, make sure that you keep it small and practical.

DEVELOPING A ROUTINE THAT WORKS FOR YOU

Although I recommend that every golfer should follow the process of "filling up the bottle" that I have just highlighted, what happens next will differ from individual to individual. There is no generic pre-shot routine that is suitable for all golfers simply because no two golfers are the same. Feel-orientated players, for example, will prefer to develop a sensation of what their body should be doing during the swing to create a specific type of shot, while visual golfers are more likely to hold an image of the shot they want to play in their mind. In addition to these two types of golfer, there are many players who like to combine elements of both visualization and feel into their routine.

There is no generic pre-shot routine that is suitable for all golfers.

Whichever routine you prefer, your first step is to understand what type of internal language your body most readily responds to. You can discover this for yourself with the use of some simple self-observation. Do pictures come readily to mind when you are asked to imagine something? Do you often speak in terms of feeling something or seeing something? Is using swing keys or thoughts an important element of your game? Would you find it easy or difficult to describe a shot before you played it? Asking yourself questions such as these will help you to work out which is the most effective method of self-communication for you.

ROUTINE 1: THE SWING REHEARSAL ROUTINE

If you are more of a feel player, the "rehearsal" routine is likely to be most suitable for you. If you find visualization difficult, or if your brain communicates with you through a sense of motion or feelings rather than images, then it is through this medium that your swing must be communicated to your body and consequently, routine 2 may be more suited to your game.

Quality feedback is the key to any "rehearsal" routine, whether it is used in the long or the short game. This entire routine is based upon the theory that your body is like a sponge and will soak up the physical feelings associated with movements, assess and then interpret them.

For example, how many times have you hit a poor shot during a casual round of golf, immediately thrown down another ball and then hit a great one? Your second swing felt much better and more controlled, your balance was good and your strike felt solid and powerful. Why was this? The answer is quite simply that your body was given a second chance to improve upon its first attempt.

Golfers who rely on feel will play their best when they incorporate an accurate physical key during their swing—one very simple swing thought to focus the mind. I say "accurate" only because you cannot hide from any physical or technical limitations that you may possess. If there is a fault in your swing it will remain there until the issue has been resolved. This fact highlights the benefit of seeking a coach who can quickly identify and remedy any swing flaws, while furnishing you with a simple thought or feeling that is practical enough to take onto the golf course.

THE SWING REHEARSAL

Once you have "filled up your bottle," the next step is to stand beside the ball and rehearse one of two things. You can either rehearse the swing you need for the shape of shot you wish to produce, or focus on the one key feeling that you feel your swing requires. Whichever rehearsal you choose, however, your practice swing next to the ball must accurately represent the swing you intend to make for real. It must have the same rhythm, the same shape and, most importantly, it must have the same overall feeling.

I do not recommend that you make a set number of practice swings each time, but, during a match, any more than two is impractical and close to becoming a breach of etiquette. On the range, however, feel free to make as many swing rehearsals as necessary, since the more time you can spend on your routine in practice, the more instinctive it will become on the course.

If there is one area of the swing that you should really pay attention to during this rehearsal stage it is the feeling created through impact and beyond. Since this is the moment of truth in the golf swing, try to absorb as much detail and information as possible. Try closing your eyes as you make these practice swings to intensify the feelings.

One important point to remember is that once you have "captured" the feelings of the swing you want to make, you should not wait too long before hitting the shot. The sensations that you generate with your practice swing will fade the longer you spend away from the ball.

Get into your set-up, pull the trigger and go!

Finally, your body and mind always reflect on what they have just experienced, but this feedback is only available if you are receptive to it. The rehearsal routine is perfect for the golfer who needs to feel right before hitting the shot.

THE REHEARSAL
ROUTINE—SENSING
EVERYTHING THAT
YOU NEED AND
WANT FROM
YOUR SWING.

ROUTINE 2: THE VISUAL ROUTINE

If you are blessed with the ability to visualize in your mind anything that you desire, you are also lucky enough to have one of the greatest gifts of golf. Even if you are a "feel" player, it is still a worthwhile exercise to practice the art of creating pictures in the mind as they can provide clarity and focus that few other skills can match.

If you are a visual player, you will probably find that some shots come to you far more easily than others. These are the shots that you have already achieved a certain degree of success with and are therefore stored in the brain ready for instant reference. Other shots, however, need to be worked at. Even the most accomplished artist has days when they experience difficulty in planning their next composition. If you find a certain shot difficult to visualize in your mind, you have to work at it. The answer is there if you just ask the right questions.

1 Where do I want the ball to start?

This is the first and most important question that you need to ask yourself. It is always a good idea to plan on creating a little movement in the air with the ball if only because the dead straight shot is the most difficult to produce in golf. Your intended shape can be the result of either your natural tendency to move the ball in a certain direction or as a conscious effort to do so. Shaping the ball in a controlled fashion also offers a greater margin for error. Moving the ball from one side of the fairway to the other, for example, allows you to use the full width of the fairway, whereas a straight shot only has half the fairway to use before running into trouble.

2 Selecting a specific target

Common sense dictates that if you want an accurate result, you should choose an accurate target. The golfer who is just satisfied to aim somewhere in the general vicinity of the green, for example, cannot realistically expect to land the ball next to the flag. The golfer who asks a better question of the shot he is about to play, selects a precise target and designates a certain route to the pin can rightly expect a slightly more pleasing result.

A general target will not grab and hold your attention like a small, precise or interesting target. Look at how these trees have provided naturally small targets to choose from as they form a silhouette against the light. Clouds can also be interesting and useful targets. However, it goes without saying that a target should be practical enough in size to ensure that you do not lose it as you are over the ball. The credo for targeting is to work in inches and not yards. The two examples shown are just a couple of ways that you can bring a target to life so that it resonates in the mind.

TWO EXAMPLES OF SHOT TARGETS: THE SILHOUETTES OF TREES
FORMED AGAINST THE LIGHT PROVIDE NATURALLY SMALL TARGETS,
WHILE A CLOUD MAKES THE PERFECT HIGH-SHOT TARGET.

3 Identify your finishing target

It stands to reason that your starting target should be more specific than your finishing target, since if the ball does not start out on the correct line there is very little, if any, chance of it reaching its intended destination. The finishing target is important in that it finalizes your game plan for the shot. You can define the final destination of the ball in your mind by visualizing it nestling next to the pin or in a designated position in the fairway.

THE 7 LAWS OF THE GOLF SWING

PRACTICE EXERCISE: LEARN TO HOLD THE TARGET

The benefit of selecting an interesting target—or one that you can make interesting—should now be apparent. You should be looking for a striking target on the golf course that readily imprints itself on your memory.

When you go to see a film, the action-packed last 10 minutes ensure that you leave the cinema with these final scenes imprinted in your memory. You should be looking for a similar, long-lasting effect with the target you identify on the golf course.

As this image shows, the visually aware golfer should have the ability to retain the image of the starting target in his mind even as his head returns to look back down at the ball. Practice this now. Take a moment to look at something in the room or out of the window, remembering to make it specific. As soon as you have seen something that catches your eye, turn the other way or close your eyes and see if you can still hold the image in your mind. If you can, then you also have the ability to "hold on" to your target as you look at the ball. Start off by hitting a few putts with this technique followed by some chips and pitches. You will soon find that the mind grows quieter when it becomes occupied with something more specific.

LEARN TO HOLD THE TARGET ▶
IMAGE IN YOUR MIND ONCE
YOUR EYES HAVE RETURNED
TO THE BALL.

THE WAGGLE—YOUR LINK BETWEEN THE SET-UP AND THE SWING

Up to this point there has been very little motion in either of the two recommended pre-shot routines. To create a good rhythm you must effectively jump start your swing into action. The bridge between your address position and your swing is the "waggle."

It's my guess that even as you hear the word "waggle," you are tempted to dismiss this feature of the golf swing as some kind of optional extra that you can quite easily do without. The fact is, however, that a good waggle will instigate and create a flow to your swing in a more effective way than any other method. The waggle fulfils two very important functions. The first is to create rhythm and the second is to rehearse the desired move away from the ball.

USING YOUR WAGGLE TO CREATE MOTION

Unlike sports such as tennis or squash, where the body instinctively reacts to the movement of the ball, in golf the ball sits on the ground waiting to be hit and, therefore, there is no movement to trigger the swing. The waggle performs this task for you by creating the signal for your swing to jump into gear.

▼ SETTLED AND READY FOR MOTION.

▼ START TO WAGGLE AND FLOW.

The best kind of waggle incorporates an effective use of the eyes. As you can see from this image, the waggle actually takes place as you focus on the target. In this case, returning the clubface and your eyes to the ball is the trigger that enables you to instantly start your backswing. This denies the mind both the time and the opportunity to entertain any negative thoughts, and at the same time ensures that your final look at the target remains fresh and vivid.

USE YOUR WAGGLE AS A BACKSWING REHEARSAL

In addition to injecting motion into your swing, the waggle can also be used as a primer for the swing motion. Ideally, the waggle should be a small rehearsal of the wrist action that is required to set the club on the correct plane in the backswing. This abbreviated movement should take the clubhead to a point opposite the right foot.

Some players believe that a slightly longer waggle allows them to generate a little more flow and rhythm. In this case, the right wrist will hinge a little more to a point where the shaft of the club finishes directly over the toe line and with the leading edge of the clubface pointing upwards. Both variations of the waggle are an effective and appropriate rehearsal for the real swing.

▼ HEAD AND CLUB RETURN TOGETHER.

▼ REACT AND START YOUR SWING.

HAVING MOTION TO CREATE MOTION

It is a common misbelief that the set-up position is a static one. As far as good, experienced players are concerned, that could not be further from the truth. The world's top players are "alive" at address for the one simple reason that it is very difficult to make a smooth and rhythmical swing from a totally still position.

Some players are born with the ability to create motion over the ball; others need to work at it. You do, however, have the opportunity to design the exact type of pre-swing motion that you want. The most effective way of achieving this is to watch good players on television. It won't be too long before you find a player whose mannerisms and pre-swing motions look familiar to you in terms of what you would like to achieve in your own set-up. Simply go ahead and copy them or use their routine as a foundation for creating your own unique motion.

LEARNING TO LET GO OF CONTROL

When you allow your routine to flow and your body to respond instinctively to your pre-swing trigger, you will experience the feeling of letting go of the previous inhibitions that you believed allowed you to control your swing. For some golfers, this feeling of losing control can be quite daunting, especially if you have been guilty of consciously "working" your golf swing. Get used to this liberating feeling and enjoy it. The ability to let go and trust your swing within the framework of a well-orchestrated pre-shot routine can help you overcome many of golf's difficult situations, such as first-tee nerves, pressure shots and competitive matches.

MAKING EYE CONTACT—THE FIRST STEP OF A BEAUTIFUL BALL-TO-TARGET RELATIONSHIP

Your eyes are always your biggest assets on the golf course because they provide the body with its most valuable stimuli. Top class tournament professionals will use their eyes to ascertain the direction of the wind by observing movement in the trees or by the movement of the ripples in a nearby water hazard. They will also look for subtle, yet vital, information on the greens, such as the direction of the grain or the break of a putt. This attention to detail in each and every shot is one of the key factors that separates the professional from the amateur golfer.

To reach your full potential as a golfer, you must learn to use your eyes effectively.

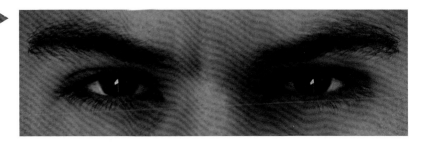

Your own on-course strategy can be changed or saved by using your eyes correctly. Paying attention to how a playing partner's putt rolls on the green, for example, will give you vital clues as to how your own putt will break. It really is this simple: to reach your full potential as a golfer you must learn to effectively use your eyes. Regardless of whether you are a kinesthetic (feel) golfer or more of a visual player, you must have a basic understanding of what is expected from your eyes.

For example, it is futile to stand on the tee looking down the fairway trying to ignore a water hazard that flanks the entire left side of the hole. Simply pretending that the water doesn't exist will not work, by trying to persuade yourself that the water is simply not there, you merely strengthen its presence in your mind. A more effective course of action is to take in as much detail as possible and then work out a strategy that takes the hazard out of the equation.

WHAT YOU SEE IS NOT ALWAYS WHAT YOU GET

While you are totally reliant on the information provided by your eyes to make the correct decisions on the golf course, remember that your eyes can sometimes deceive you. In golf, what you see is not always what you get!

Many golf course architects are masters at using the effects of bunkering and elevation changes to disguise hazards and create optical illusions that can, for example, foreshorten the distance to the target or give the impression of a tight landing making it difficult to select the correct club and line.

A golf hole that looks very intimidating from the tee can look absolutely benign when viewed from the opposite angle. With this in mind, many tournament golfers will actually walk a new golf course backwards during practice in order to obtain a better perspective on the difficulty of the hole and to develop an effective strategy for the hole in question.

On the shorter holes and par-3s, the course architect will often try to create confusion in a golfer's mind by placing a large bunker 20 to 30 yards short of the green. This design effect makes the hole look longer than it actually is, so always go by the yardage on the tee marker in such instances.

USE YOUR EYES LIKE A CAMERA LENS

I encourage my pupils—both amateur and professional—to use their eyes in the same way that a photographer would adjust the lens on a camera. You can either use a zoom lens to narrow your focus onto a small target in the distance and to blur out distractions to reduce your margin for error, or use a wide-angle lens that broadens your focus and allows you to take in more of the scenery around you in order to help you relax and lower your concentration levels.

FOR ULTIMATE ACCURACY, BURN THE FLAG

The image of burning a flag through the sheer intensity of narrowing your focus should give you a good idea of what I mean by reducing your margin for error. In selecting a distinctive target you not only outline a definite strategy for the shot that you are about to play, you also subconsciously instruct your brain to achieve the desired outcome.

If you define your target specifically enough with your eyes, the brain will go to great lengths in order to provide the end result that you want. If you have no clear goal for the direction of the ball, you have little hope for a favorable outcome.

POSITIVE AND EFFECTIVE SELF-TALK— YOU ARE WHAT YOU SAY

There is an old saying that says: "A man becomes what he thinks about all day." One of the keys to success in golf, and indeed many walks of life, is the ability to communicate effectively with one's self. In order to become a good golfer, you will need to develop this skill. This "self-talk" is nothing more than an affirmation of what you want to achieve. The adage "as you think, you become" reinforces the dramatic effect that your inner voice can have on your general behavior and life.

Instruct yourself to apply 100 percent focus and application to each and every shot.

If you continually tell yourself, for example, that you find a particular shot difficult or that a certain situation makes you uncomfortable, then this will very quickly become your reality. Fortunately, the opposite is also true. If you instruct yourself to apply 100 percent focus and application to each and every shot, it won't be long before you notice a major difference in your outlook to playing the kind of shots that you normally approach with trepidation.

USE YOUR EYES AND NARROW YOUR FOCUS TO "BURN" THE TARGET.

One particularly effective example of positive self-talk is to describe your desired shot to yourself quietly under your breath before you start your pre-shot routine. Tell yourself where you want the ball to start, where you want it to finish and what type of trajectory you would like to achieve. You can practice this exercise in relaxed social games with your friends simply by challenging each other to nominate the type of shot you are going to play before you hit the ball. Award yourselves points out of five for how closely your shots resembled your predictions. The other benefit of this exercise, of course, is that you will very soon discover which shots you are comfortable playing and those that require a little attention on the practice range.

FINDING AND STAYING IN THE ELUSIVE "ZONE"

If you are a keen golfing spectator or TV viewer, it is likely that you will have heard commentators talk about a particular player being "in the zone." This phrase refers to a state of mind that a few golfers can find some of the time, other golfers have never experienced, but that a select few seem to be able to tap into just about every time they play.

THE SEVEN STEPS ▶
TO GREAT GOLF.

When you are in this mental zone, every single target seems sharper, you have plenty of time and hitting the ball solidly seems to come naturally. However, for some strange reason, this zone is nearly impossible to recreate on a conscious level. The more you try to enter this state the more elusive it becomes. The word "trying" is particularly relevant in this context since most of the amateur golfers who have somehow found themselves in the zone have almost always stumbled blindly into it!

However, the good news is that you can greatly increase your chances of entering and remaining in the zone simply by developing a thorough, consistent and efficient pre-shot routine. There are no guarantees, but the road that takes you there is a clear one. For this mental zone to be experienced and enjoyed, certain key elements of your game must be harmonious. You must be physically competent, you must be deeply relaxed yet focused, and the challenge facing you must grab your full attention. The general rule is that the quieter the mind, the greater the likelihood of these elements combining together.

SEVEN SMALL STEPS TO GREAT CONCENTRATION

During an average round of golf, you will probably find yourself on the course for somewhere in the region of four hours. Although good concentration is a vital ingredient in the recipe for consistent and successful golf, it is quite simply impossible to remain intense and focused for this length of time.

The image on page 167 represents your concentration zone. It is a small corridor of approximately seven steps (three and a half on either side of the ball), and it is the only time on the golf course that you should concern yourself with the shot in hand. Once you are outside this boundary, feel free to let your mind wander, talk with playing partners or simply enjoy the scenery.

The first element of the image shows a golfer immediately after he has conducted his analysis or assessment and has decided what type of shot he wants to play. At this stage, the player is about to initiate his physical trigger in order to switch off the conscious mind. For optimum efficiency and effectiveness, there should be very little, if any conscious thought present in the mind as you make your swing. Your ultimate goal is to create an habitual golf swing. This is represented by the middle image.

As the golfer leaves the hitting area, he or she should be experiencing a mental closure to the shot. Irrespective of the result—good or bad—you must endeavor not to carry your emotions forward with you beyond the seventh step. Every great golfer has had the ability to remain in the present and not to dwell on past errors, but this is an area of the game where most of us have plenty of room for improvement.

SUMMARY

The beauty of Law 7 is its flexibility. As a tool for creating robust and reliable habits to use on the golf course it still needs to retain a level of flexibility to take into account the unpredictability of the human element. This does not mean that you should take this law less seriously than the others, however. It is not, by any stretch of the imagination, a poor relation. It is, in fact, the Godfather of the swing.

There will be times on the golf course when too many competing and sometimes conflicting swing thoughts will threaten to clog your mind. There will also be times when your nerves try their hardest to get the better of you. The course may be beating you up or inclement weather conditions may be clouding your judgement. It is important to remember that these experiences can and will happen, so you have to be prepared for them and know how to act as and when they surface.

So what do you do? The one thing you must not do at any cost is abandon this law. It acts as a beacon for the mind and body when experiencing a difficult moment on the golf course. Trust in it more and delve deeper into its content. The truly great players have the ability to immerse themselves completely in the moment and block out anything that might induce a negative thought or feeling. This powerful state of mind starts with the process of "filling up the bottle" on page 148, in which the assessment of the shot and the subsequent process of absorption begins.

In the future, it will be the content and subject matter of Law 7 plus the spiritual balance of human nature that will help golfers the world over take the next step in their pursuit of golfing excellence. The detail may change, but the goal of creating total harmony between mind and body will not. While an enhanced understanding of the body's biomechanics will eventually remove the mystery and inaccurate guesswork associated with the swing technique, there are so many untapped resources to discover within the hidden chambers of the mind that the prospect of the kind of golf to come is nothing less than mouth-watering.

During the last century we have seen many well-known golfers with the ability to adopt Law 7 as an integral part of their own body and psyche. The common denominator that links players such as Ben Hogan, Jack Nicklaus, Nick Faldo and Tiger Woods is a total trust and clarity in their physical and mental ability to carry out the job in hand. Do not just read this chapter and then forget it, make this law an integral part of every golf ball you strike. That is the first step to true commitment.

GOLF SWING NAVIGATION TOOL

LAW 1 QUESTIONS

1   The feeling of my grip seems to change from day to day. Why is this so inconsistent?
2   Since you cannot see grip pressure, what should I be sensing if I am in doubt of its quality?
3   I continually get golfer's elbow. What is the cause of this?
4   I do my best and feel that I "fill up the bottle," but my shots can still fly off-line. How do I start to put this right?

LAW 1 ANSWERS

1   You must look at the routine you employ to place the hands onto the grip of the club. It is likely that this varies from shot to shot. Go back to Law 1 and study the introduction of the club into the left hand and the continuing role that the right hand can play.

2   The pressure of the grip should govern the movement of the hands while encouraging the proper energy and mobility to move the club with authority. Use the image of gas gently escaping from the grip (page 29) to help with this. Too tight and nothing escapes, too loose and slack and you'll get a deluge!

3   The majority of tendon-related injuries emanate from a faulty hold on the club. Specifically you should look to the "long left thumb" (page 20) which has the effect of lengthening the tendons of the left arm until they become taught and stretched. When impact occurs these tendons become plucked—rather like the strings on a guitar, thus aggravating the connection sockets attached to the bone.

4   If your swing follows a good path and you feel that your pre-shot routine is detailed enough, it sounds like your grip warrants attention. Check the positional equality of both hands relative to the head of the club (page 22).

LAW 2 QUESTIONS

1   How far should my arms hang from my body?
2   My swing always feels loose and I can never finish in a balanced position. What is causing this?
3   I feel that I am making great progress with my swing but I still hit some poor strikes. What am I missing?
4   As I approach the back nine my lower back always starts to ache and gets progressively worse. What is the likely cause?

LAW 2 ANSWERS

1   The key to creating this arm/body relationship is knowing what to feel and where. To answer this, hold your arms horizontally out in front of you from a standing position. Now clap your hands together and start to move your arms in slowly toward your chest. When you sense a light pressure between your upper arms and your body you have created the correct relationship between the two.

2   This answer is twofold. Firstly, your swing becomes long due to the fact that your base provides no stability for your body motion and your arm-swing. Go back to "strength from stability" (page 33) and copy the leg positions in the images provided. Balance is also created for the legs and their relationship with the upper body. Ensure that your torso does not hang too far out from the toes or sit too far back onto the heels.

3   The poor strikes you experience are likely to come from your ball position/sternum position at the time of impact. Use the information supplied in the "ball position" section (page 34) and a mirror to increase your chances of a pure strike.

4   The lower back pain that you experience is likely to be the muscles in the lower back straining under the load of the torso. You must ensure that your posture is sharp. You do this by creating the two curves in the lower and upper spine. As your round goes on the aching pain increases in carrying the heavy load. Go back to "two key curves to preserve" (page 39) and remember that the spine is the body's coat hanger, so use it!

LAW 3 QUESTIONS

1   Why is such a small detail such as the right foot position at address crucial to good leg action?

2   I always work on squatting into and loading up my right leg but I still over-swing, why is this?

3   My divots are either thin or too deep and affect my strike, what is going wrong?

4   Try as I might, I still cannot get that "loaded" look all the professionals get into at the top of the swing, what should I focus on?

LAW 3 ANSWERS

1   The positioning of the feet can ultimately affect the movement of the hip and torso action. We need the torso to rotate, not tilt during both the backswing and the downswing. This is encouraged when both feet are slightly turned outward. Having the right foot square can also exacerbate knee and cartilage problems.

2   You need to focus a little more on the motion of the left leg. Remember that the golf swing involves both sides of the body, each playing vital roles at different times. Adopt the "left leg drill" (page 60) into your practice sessions and you will notice a difference.

3   The inconsistency of your divot pattern starts with the backswing and downswing movement of your torso. It is likely that you are tilting your hips during the swing thus altering the depth of the following hit. This fault also affects golfers who top the ball. You should work on achieving a "level belt line" (page 66).

4   If you are not getting behind the ball on the completion of your backswing you should first check that the dorsal aspect of your set-up position is correct (page 43).

LAW 4 QUESTIONS

1 I have tried to hinge and re-hinge and copy the feather image but I still fail to copy the set positions.

2 I have heard that if the club is too "narrow" on the way down I should "throw" the club into the ball from the top, is this good?

3 I always have a "drop kick" hit with my driver and seem to duff my irons, what is happening?

4 I have read in magazines that a wide and slow backswing is the perfect way to start your backswing, is this right?

LAW 4 ANSWERS

1 It is very likely that the handle of the club is riding high in the palm of your left hand. This drastically reduces the chance of motion in the wrist bone as the handle of the club interferes with the capitate joint. Go back to Law 1 and look toward the dual role that the right hand can provide while introducing it into the left.

2 "Throwing" the club from the top of the swing to prevent a narrow downswing can in some cases prove successful. However, what must accompany this is the right side firing though the ball.

3 These types of strike are typical of the golfer who casts the club like a fishing rod early into the downswing. You must lighten up your grip and appreciate the swinging weight of the club. Go back and study the "whip" image (page 91) to achieve this sensation.

4 The best golf swings will always represent a small and fast circle (relative to the body speed) around the body. A long, wide and slow motion will only create a great strain on the timing relationships between the body, arms and ultimately the clubhead.

LAW 5 QUESTIONS

1   I have always struggled with the shape of the first part of my backswing.

2   Should the clubhead point at the target at the top of the swing?

3   I always seem to over-swing thus never achieving the "Line of Fire" completion plane.

4   My through plane always looks high and right despite my attempts to "round it off," what is going wrong?

LAW 5 ANSWERS

1   There are two aspects you should check. Number one—ensure that your hands have positional equality on the handle of the golf club. A grip that displays positional weakness or strength will dominate this first stage of the swing. Number two—make sure that you develop a waggle that mirrors the takeaway you want to achieve. It is likely that the clubhead has become overly influenced by the body early on.

2   No. If the clubhead points directly at the target at the top of the backswing it is in fact off-plane. Remember that the golf swing is not a straight line but an ellipse, having the club point at the target would encourage blocks and hooks.

3   You will need to re-read and employ the "moon crescent" drill (page 87) to gain a better linkage between the body and the arms. When the tension in the arms is different than that of the body gaining the correct club positions is difficult.

4   When your through-swing plane is high you must first look towards your downswing body motion and then towards your arm action. It is highly likely that the starting point of this problem starts with all the tendencies associated with the "Reverse C" fault. As the left side of the body lifts and tilts, the arms are automatically thrown up, high and away from the body. Try hitting some half shots with a glove held under your left armpit while maintaining your spine angle into your follow-through.

LAW 6 QUESTIONS

1   What starts the downswing?
2   My poor shot is topping the ball, what should I focus on?
3   Why should I practice my follow-through when my swing has effectively finished?
4   I have always wanted my tempo to be slower. I can do this for a few holes but I always revert
     back to a quicker swing.

LAW 6 ANSWERS

1   The start of the downswing is already in your grasp. The pattern of the downswing is identi-
     cal to that of walking. Do not analyze this area of your golf swing. Carry out and repeat the
     "step in" drill (page 127), it will answer all of your questions.

2   When you top the ball, two main aspects of the swing have been neglected. The first is your
     spine angle. Once created at address you must maintain the spine angle until the ball is well
     on its way. It is likely that your right side will not be firing through the ball either. Work on
     these two simultaneously and you will see the difference it can make.

3   The follow-through is representative of what has gone on before it. Practicing a great follow-
     through can often give you an insight into an earlier stage of your swing, so do not dismiss it.

4   Remember that the speed of your golf swing is closely linked to your personality and
     size. Copy a golfer who is of a similar stature and temperament to you, and you will have
     more success.

LAW 7 QUESTIONS

1   Swing thought or no swing thought, what is the answer?
2   I use the "rehearsal" routine in my short game which works well, but it doesn't transfer to my long game well. Why?
3   I ALWAYS work on my routine but can never get settled. What is going wrong?
4   When I am in the "zone" I can hit great shots, but I can revert back to a conscious state, why?

LAW 7 ANSWERS

1   If you are analytical and process information verbally then you will play best with ONE very simple swing thought. However, if you have strong visual and kinesthetic (feel) tendencies, you should encourage your mind to be silent.

2   The "rehearsal" routine works well in your short game because there is only a brief time delay between the rehearsal and the actual stroke. Remember, do not hang around in your long game between these two periods. You must capture and use the feeling while it is still "ripe."

3   Beyond "filling up the bottle" there is little else to do in a routine. If you are always working on your routine you are giving your body no time to adopt and own it. Settle on one routine and then switch off your mind and TRUST!

4   The more you practice this submissive state, the more willingly you will enter it. Be patient and persevere.

KEY SWING SUMMARY POINTS

THE GRIP

- Remember that you should always build the grip around the "natural" hanging positions of the hands.
- Both hands are slightly inverted toward the body. You must preserve this relationship when forming your grip.
- A great grip should display a positional equality. If the left hand turns in a quarter, so must the right.
- Efficient and long-lasting golf swings are built on this foundation. Missing out or neglecting simple aspects of the grip can lead to unending frustration.

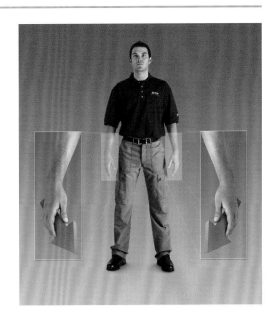

- The capitate joint dictates the amount of motion available to the wrists and hands.
- If the handle of the golf club rides high in the left palm and intrudes into the area of the capitate, leverage and timing will suffer.
- A long left thumb will also encourage the club to ride high into the palm as it assumes a weak, slice-inducing position.
- The introduction of a grip routine ensures the repetition of a good, consistent hold on the club.

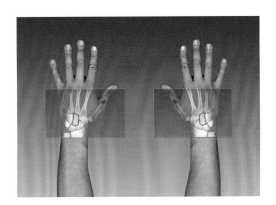

- Always introduce the handle of the club to the left hand from a north-easterly angle.
- Doing this negates the need to manipulate the left hand to fit correctly onto the grip in a neutral fashion.
- Rather than forming your grip while beside the ball, form it away from the ball. Only make your approach when you are completely happy with the feel and the position of your grip.
- As you grow more confident with your grip routine, maintain your visual relationship and "eye up" the target while forming your hold.

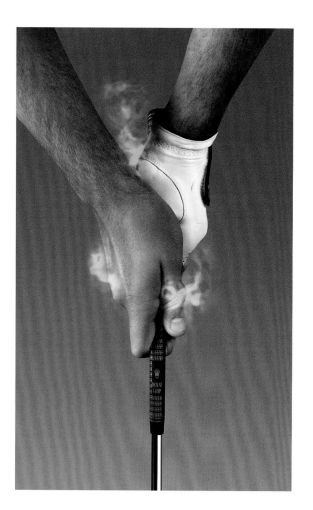

- Understand that to hit the ball hard we do not have to hold the club tightly.
- Poorly positioned grips encourage a stranglehold on the club in order to gain some sort of control. Getting it correct from the start is crucial.
- You must acquire the delicate balance between discipline and freedom in order to get the best from your grip.
- Allowing the "gas" inside the grip to intermittently seep away will encourage the correct pressure. Too tight and nothing is released, too slack and a deluge of gas escapes.

THE GEOMETRY OF THE SET-UP

- The torque and the balance present in a good golf swing require a strong base to operate from. The correct set-up achieves this through its relationship with the ground.
- Both feet should assume a slightly fanned-out position when addressing the ball to accommodate the rotation of the mid-section during the swing.
- The strongest position the legs can assume is one where the knees are directly over the feet. Evidence of this can be seen in karate and fencing.
- Make sure that your weight is spread between the balls of your feet and your heels. Similarly strive to achieve a 50/50 distribution of weight between the right and left feet.

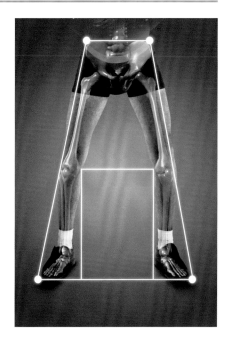

- Remember that it is preferable to adopt a "constant" ball position to promote all-round consistency and efficiency of motion.
- Once the position of the ball is determined (located by the natural hanging position of the left arm) adjacent to the left heel, their relationship must be cemented. It is the position of the right foot that varies according to the club being played.
- Take the time to understand the relationship between the sternum and the right foot. As the right foot narrows and widens the stance, the sternum must vary in its rearward and frontal tilt to guarantee the desired strike.
- The only time it is permissible for the middle of each foot to be narrower than the hip joints is when there is a displacement of weight forwards.

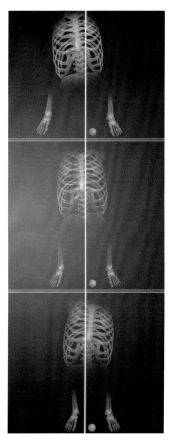

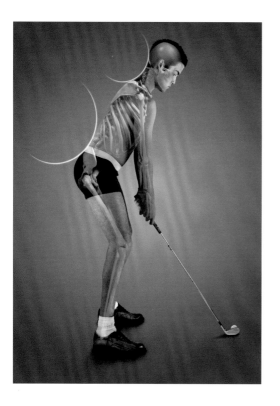

- The "feel" of the posture in golf is no different to that of a tennis player waiting to receive a serve or a karate expert poised to attack.
- There are two vital and quite natural curves we must preserve as we address the ball. The first is located at the base of the spine on the tailbone and the second can be found at the base of the neck.
- When the correct posture is present, the arms are allowed to hang from the chest in a natural and repeatable way.
- Remember that, "the spine is the coat hanger of the body." In order to avoid spinal and muscular injury, adopt the correct posture and prevent the spine sagging under the weight of the torso.

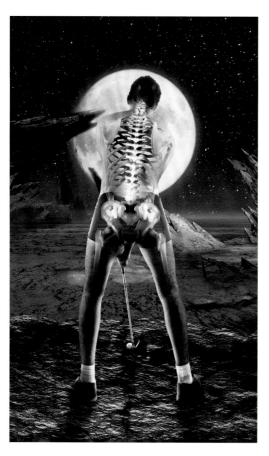

- As the head takes its Torque 2 position you should ensure total spine alignment from top to bottom. Biomechanically, this represents pure swing economy.
- The slight rearward tilt that is present in mid- and long-irons and the driver negates the need for conscious weight transference.
- The quality of the dorsal aspect visible here can only promote the very best in body motion.
- Watch out for scoliosis, this debilitating affliction affects a great number of golfers. Look out for the telltale signs mentioned in Law 2.

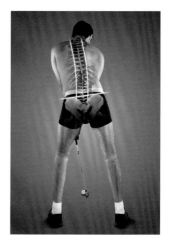

GROUNDFORCE DYNAMICS

- Learn to resist and sit into your right side, creating torque.
- The right leg drill (page 59) also ensures that the plane of the hips remains constant to the position assumed at the address position.
- The effects of an unruly body turn early on in the swing are covered in Law 4. This drill goes a long way to promoting discipline early on and sets the right tone for the rest of the swing.
- Visualize the right leg as a battery pack. The more you can load into it, the more power it will offer the golf swing.

- Truly sense the stretching sensation required to "torque up" the body in the backswing.
- The left leg drill (page 60) introduces a discipline in the body that has an immediate and positive knock-on effect on the arm-swing.
- Initially attempt the left leg drill with an 8- or 9-iron. Remember this is a stretch, so start off with some slow and deliberate swings.
- You should make the right and left leg drills a regular part of swing maintenance.

- Give your legs and body a genuine golfing workout practicing squat hits (page 63).
- If you can lower your center of gravity as you wind back, you will create tremendous torque.
- Once again the effect of working on the lower body manifests itself by disciplining the arm-swing. It will become tighter, shorter and more harmonious with the turn of the body.
- Carry out this drill with a 5- or 6-iron.

- A level belt line will promote a shallow and consistent divot pattern.
- Keeping the hip plane working in a horizontal fashion (from face on only) will ensure that all of the major joints in the body will stack up on top of each other—a must for achieving applied power into the ball.
- As the middle ground of the body, the torso has a huge responsibility to the shoulders and the knees during the swing. The directional quality of its motion is more important than the speed it creates.
- A tilted backswing and a "Reverse C" finish are by-products of mid-section rocks and sways. This poor motion also aggravates any lower back problems that may be present. Keep it level!

SYNCHRONICITY

FOCUSED MOTION

- Just as the golf swing is built from the ground upwards, the order of speed in the swing follows the same pattern.
- The speed at which certain elements of the swing travel are directly related to the distance that they have to cover.
- The golf swing has often been compared to a large cartwheel. Whilst the hub (the body) moves the slowest in its small circle, the rim (the clubhead) has to move quicker, traveling in its larger circle. The golf swing works in the same way.
- If you are having trouble with the "shape" of your golf swing, pay attention to the synchronization of it. This is where you will probably find the answer.

- To experience the correct sequencing of the backswing, first assume your regular address position.
- Close your eyes and imagine that you have a spear entering the middle of your back, through your belly button into the ball. As gruesome as this may seem, this image will help you greatly.
- As your torso is held steady by the imaginary spear, move the club back until your left arm reaches the 9 o'clock position. By this stage you should feel a slight tension in your left abdominal muscles.
- Finally, wind your body into your legs. You have just pieced together a well-timed backswing.

- A straight left arm has been a dominant swing thought in the minds of too many frustrated golfers for too long.
- To gain the proper feel of the left arm during the backswing take your regular address position.
- Take your right hand from the golf club and place it into the pocket of the elbow joint of the left arm, then allow your glove hand to swing the club back to about 9 o'clock.

- As you do this, you should sense a slight softening at the joint where your right hand is. If you have been guilty of creating tension in your left arm then this drill will be liberating for you. Once you have done this, reapply your right hand to the club and swing back encouraging the same sensation in the left arm all the way to the top of the swing.

- When the club shows efficiency in movement and works in tandem with the body it will feel as light as a feather.
- Through the proper grip (avoiding the capitate joint) start to swing, sensing little interference from the body.

- Switch your senses to your ears and listen to the pitch of the golf club orbiting around your body. If a dull sound emits from the club you are either holding the club too tightly or you have no hinge in your wrists, in which case double check the quality of your left-hand grip.
- Notice how the feather in this image appears very uniform in its movement. This occurs through the efficient hinging and re-hinging of the wrists during the swing. The "halfway back" image is mirrored by the same position halfway through. This equality of swing is desirable.

SWING PLANE

- The initial plane of the golf club away from the ball is very subtle in its shape.
- The clubface gently rotates in this arc due to a slight rotation of the forearms.
- The head remains in its Torque 1 position during these initial stages of the swing.
- The upper forearms remain closely linked to the body and resist any attempt to roll the club away from the ball.

- As you look down, your left arm should appear directly above—or slightly inverted to—your toe line.
- As you run your eyes down the shaft of the club it should point at a spot directly on the ball-to-target line.
- The leading edge of the clubface should be parallel to the angle of the shaft, indicating that it is in a neutral position.
- The body should have turned very little at this stage, thus facilitating the club's ability to find its plane.

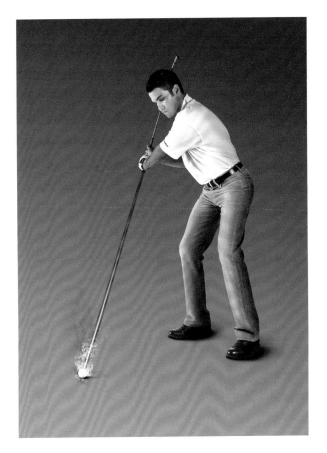

- The progression from mid to completion plane is largely completed through the turning motion of the body.
- The completion plane continues the relationship that the head of the club established at the address position by tracking a line of fire back along an extended ball-to-target line.
- The left forearm appears to cover and hide the lower part of the shoulders.
- The leading edge of the club is parallel to the left forearm.

- Past the halfway back position, the right arm will separate from the upper torso.
- This action helps to maintain the radius of the swing established at address.
- During impact and just after, the left arm gently hugs the upper torso.

- Once again the left arm separates from the body as the plane of the right arm rides up the chest into the follow-through.

FIRING INTO THE BALL

- The "step in" drill (page 127) will help you feel the transition from back-swing to downswing.
- Discover that the start of the downswing is already within your grasp.
- Take a narrow stance to the ball but ensure that the ball is positioned in the middle of the left foot.
- Make a regular backswing.
- Sensing that you are close to the end of the backswing step to the left side of the ball, thus widening your stance. Once the weight has been planted, fire through the ball with conviction and speed.

- The "Reverse C" finish is a result of a tilted mid-section and an overly aggressive leg drive. The weight almost always finishes on the back foot with the spine arched away from the target.
- When this happens, it places a positional strain upon all of the major joints in the right side of the body.
- Poor strikes, inconsistent divot patterns and a varied ball trajectory are often the result of this fault.
- If you suspect that this finish is part of your swing, check the dorsal aspect of your address followed by a review of your level belt line. It will help.

- The left side of the body prepares the hitting area while the right slams into it.
- During the backswing, the wrist and elbow joint of the right arm will close up roughly 45 degrees.
- This angle must be expelled before impact is reached for maximum power and accuracy.
- To encourage this to happen, make some swings with your right arm only. Sense that both the elbow and the wrist joints gradually open up during the downswing and resume the position they had at address.
- For total right-side release encourage the right knee to fire in at the ball at the same time as the clubhead.

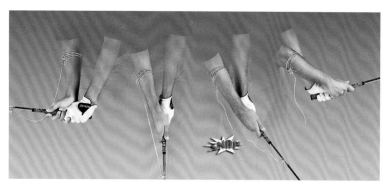

- The puck release has nothing to do with scooping the ball. Scooping only occurs when the weight and the sternum are presented way behind the ball at the moment of impact.
- Many players have talked about hitting the ball hard with the right hand. What they are referring to is the aggressive way in which you can "snap the string" (see above) from the hinged position on the downswing into the ball.
- The puck release also holds the face square to the plane for longer after impact. The hands never roll in the golf swing.
- You will find that the more a player leans back through impact (for instance in a "Reverse C" scenario), the more the hands have to compensate and bow forward through impact. Great body motion through the ball allows the golfer to release everything he has got in the correct manner.

DANCE WITH THE TARGET

- Fix your eyes on your target directly after you have finished applying your grip.
- Initiate your physical trigger by "jousting" the club firmly toward the target (see right), inducing a feeling of readiness and focus.
- Resolve to commit to the shot you are about to play.
- Welcome to "the Zone."

- Decide on the starting and finishing lines of your target.
- Stand beside the ball and make the EXACT swing you will need to execute your shot. You may want to focus on a key swing thought at this stage.
- Once you have captured the feeling, address the ball and settle in ready to go.
- Take a final look at the target and then reproduce every sense of the practice swing to create the shot you want.

- Stand roughly three and a half paces behind the ball and stare down the line of flight.
- Decide on a starting target for the ball.
- Decide on the finishing target for the ball.
- Play the shot in your mind and be sure to put in as much detail as you need. Remember, if you want an accurate outcome you must ask an accurate question.

- There are no guarantees to finding the zone as there are so many factors that must align in order to achieve this.
- However, the deeper you can immerse yourself in your routine, the greater your chances of finding it.
- View the zone as a perimeter of three and a half paces either side of the ball. Your physical trigger will turn the first key as you start your walk into the ball. A closure to the shot you have just played occurs when you have walked three and a half paces beyond where the ball lay.